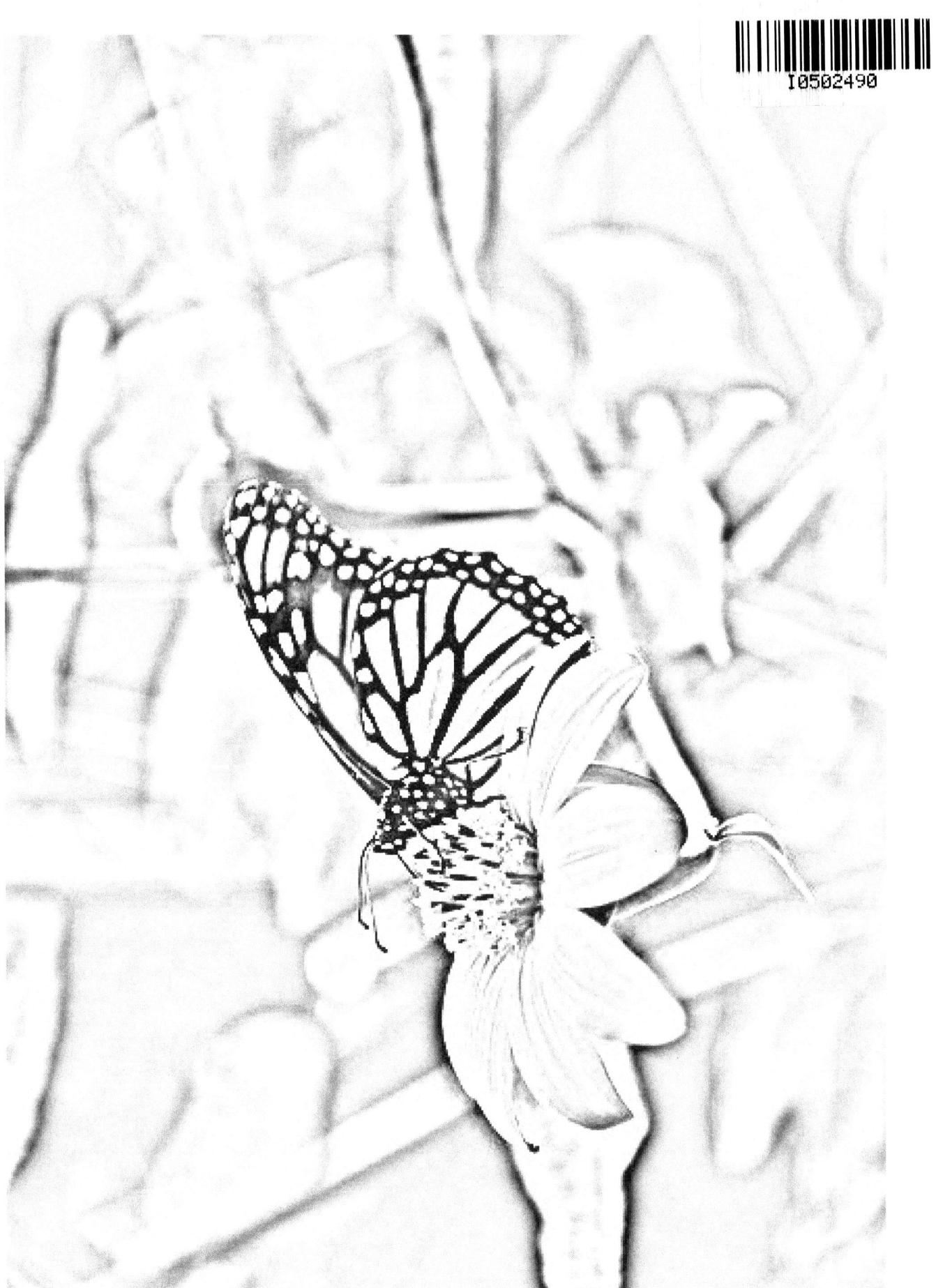

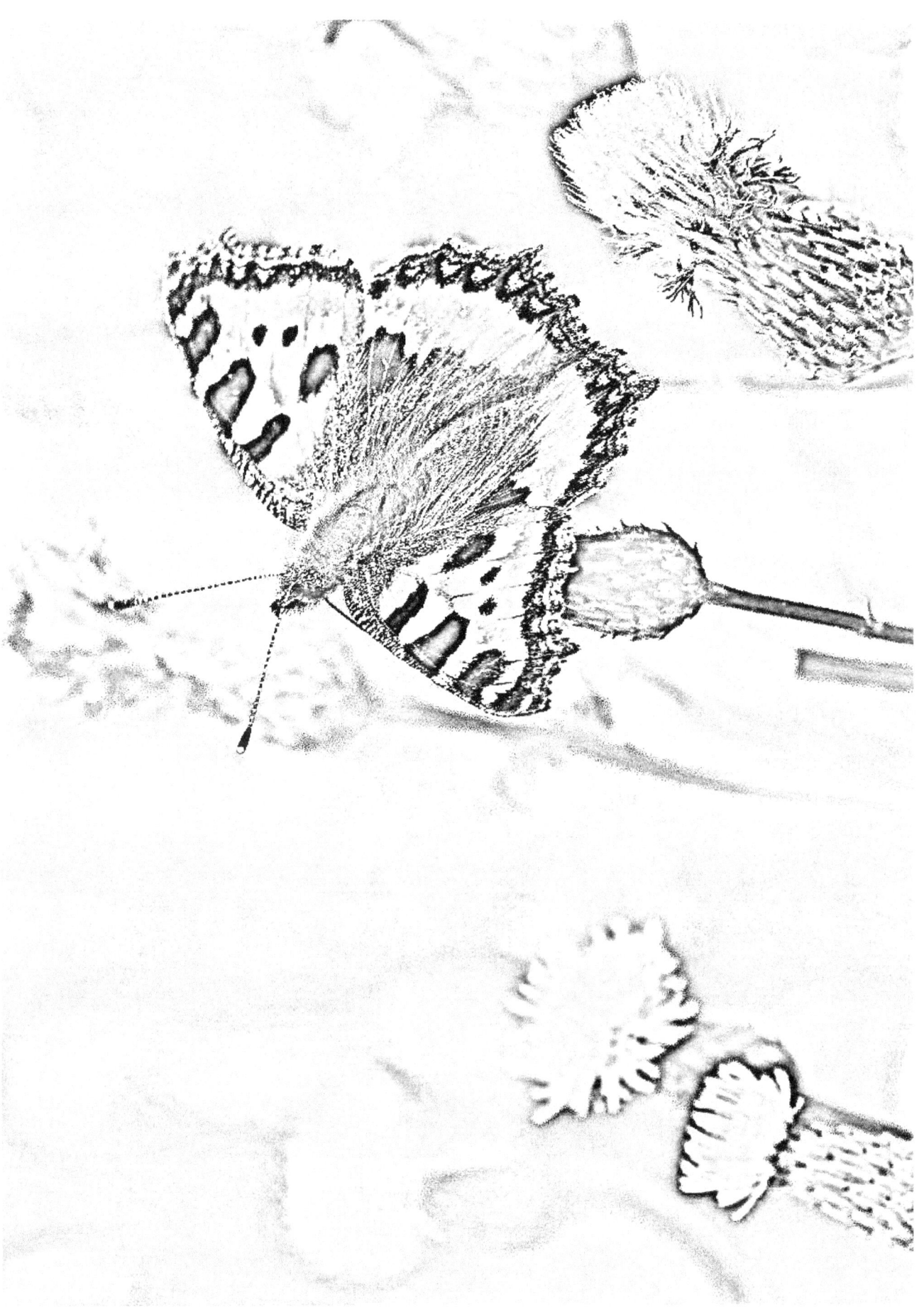

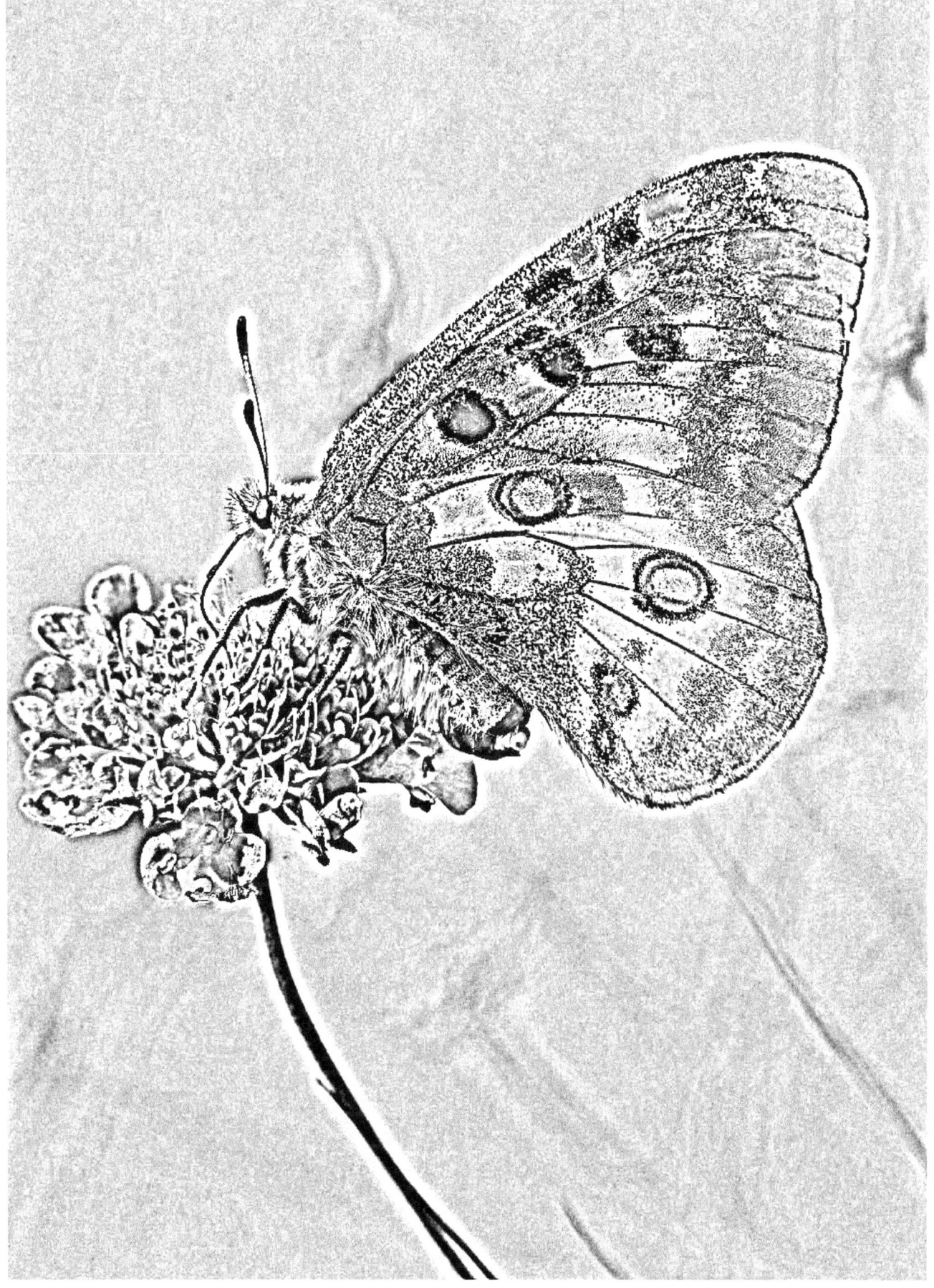

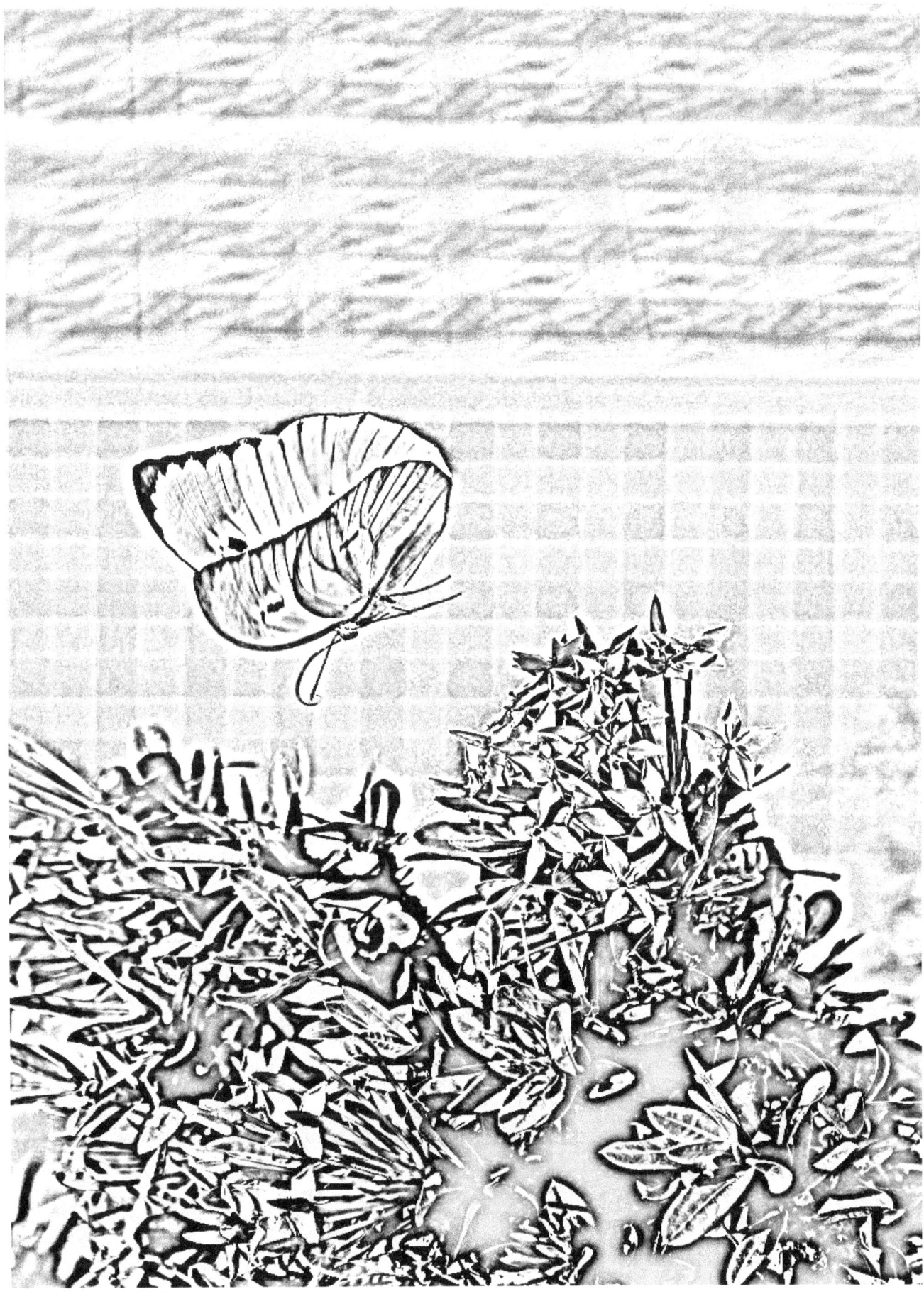

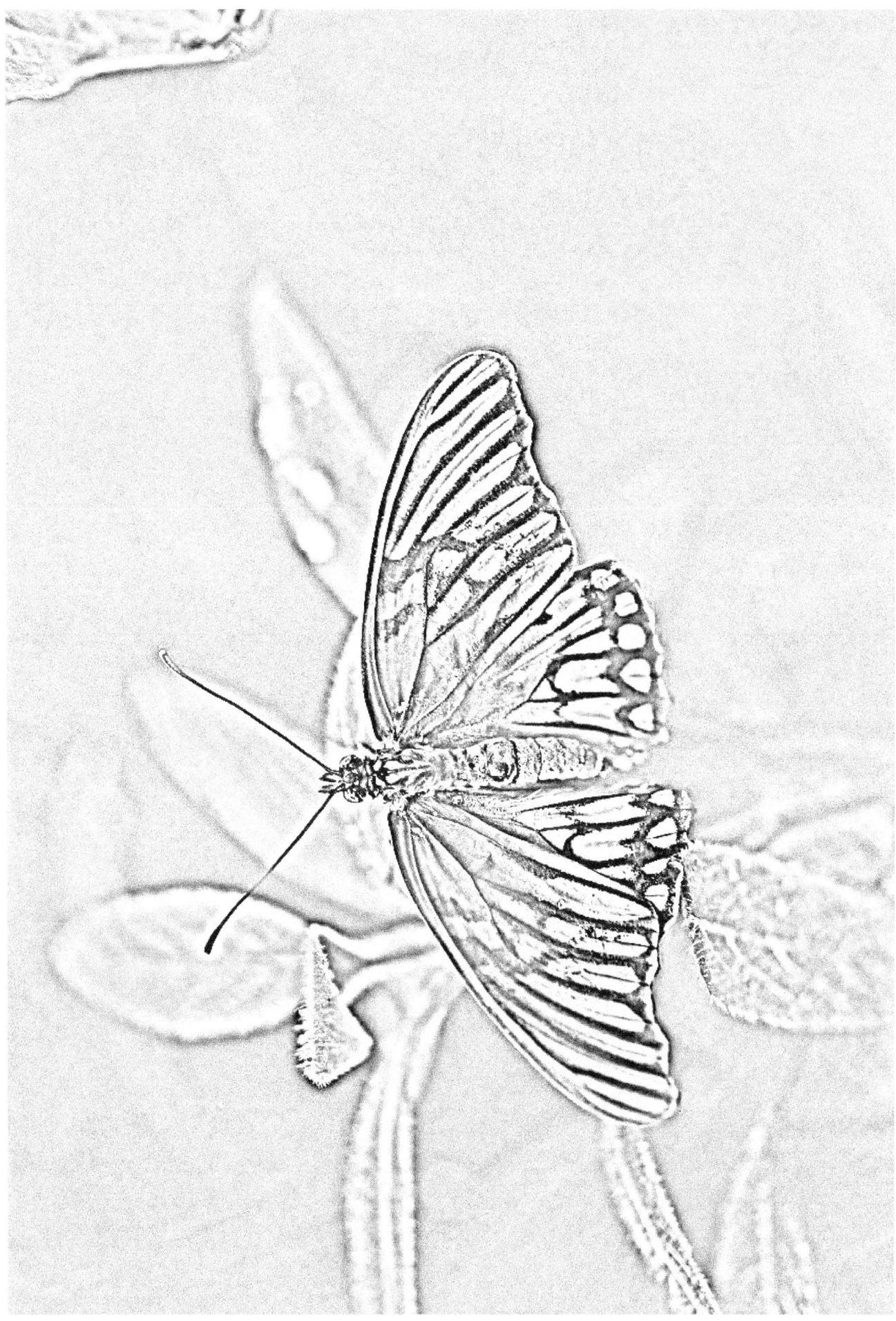

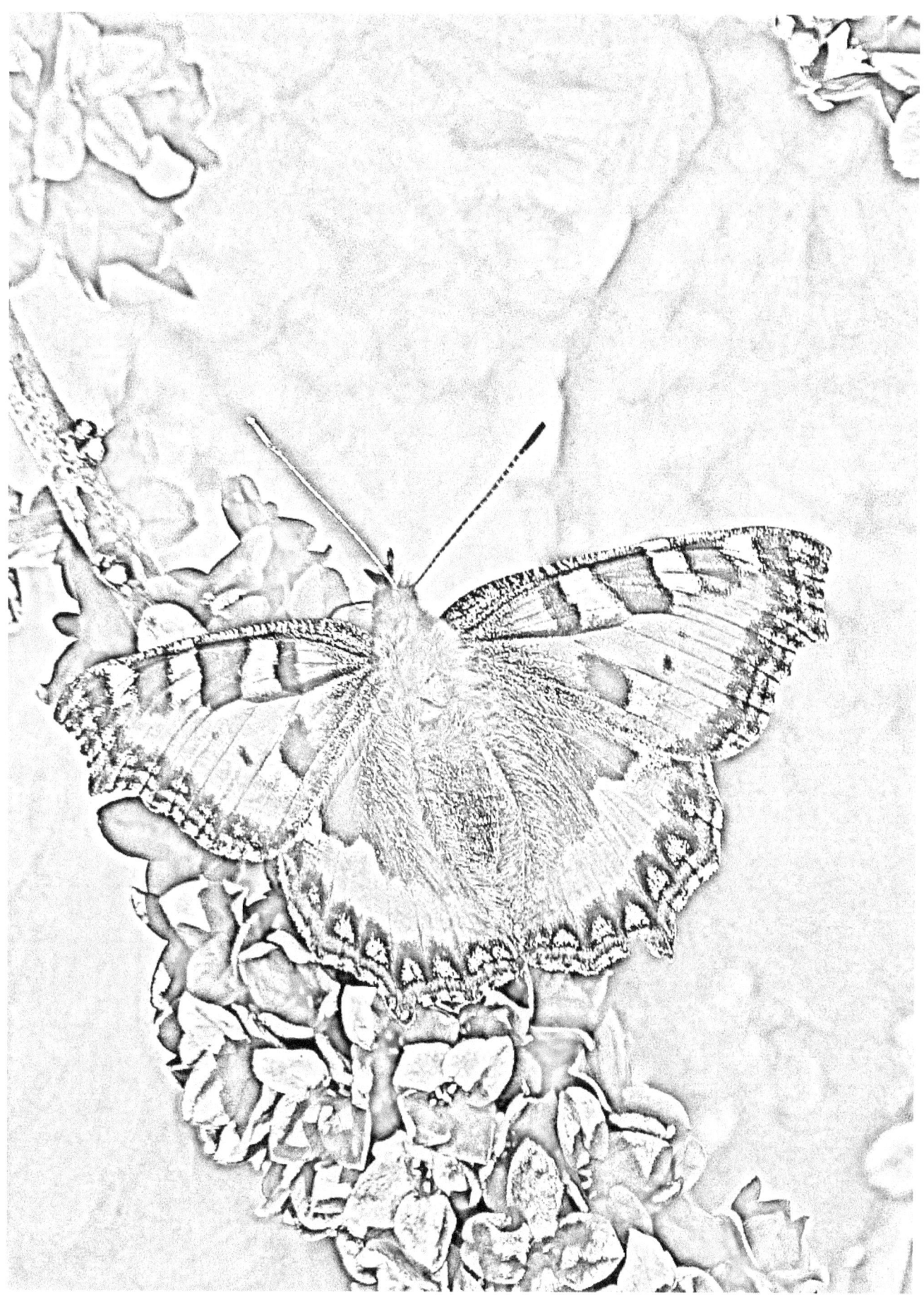

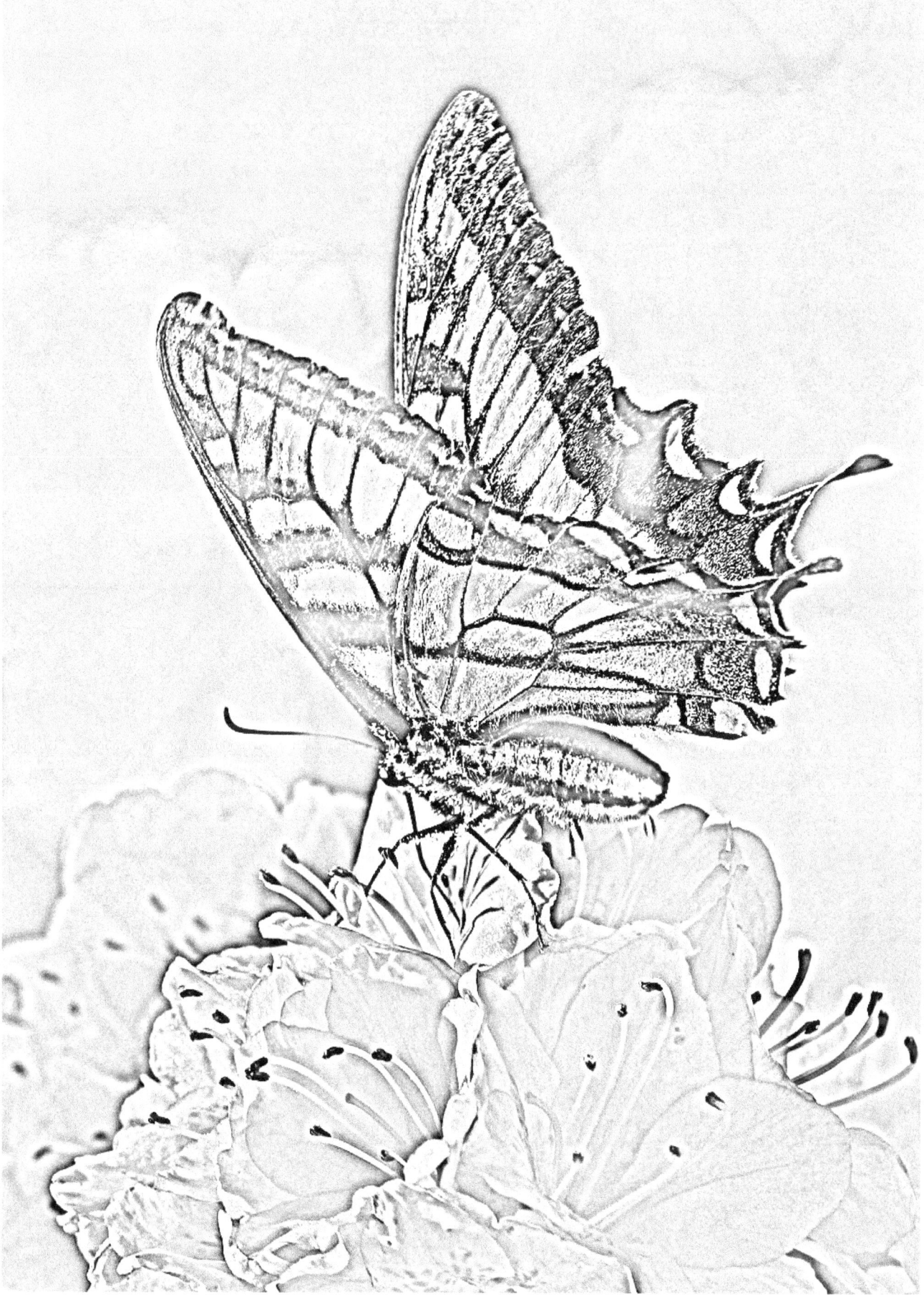

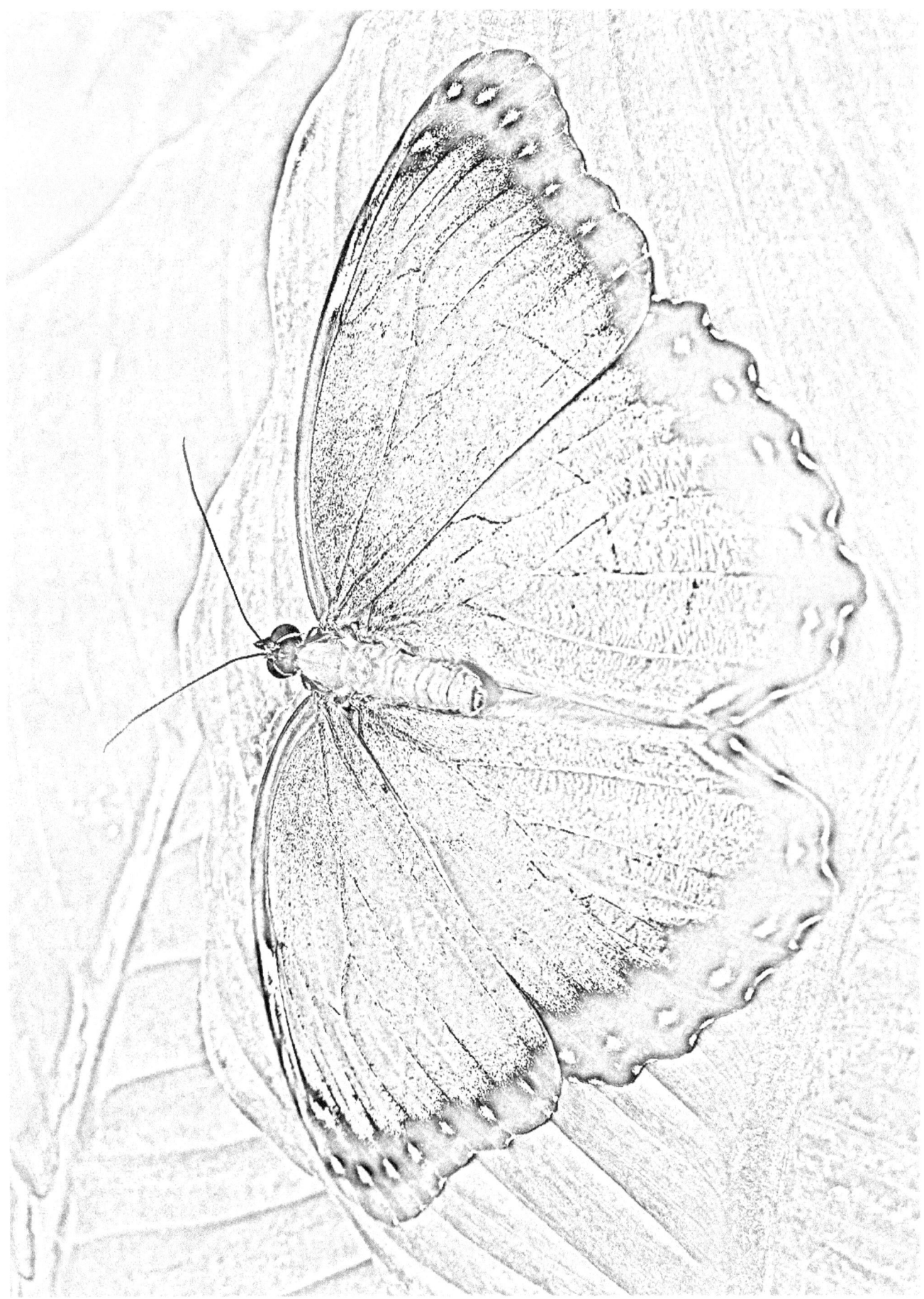

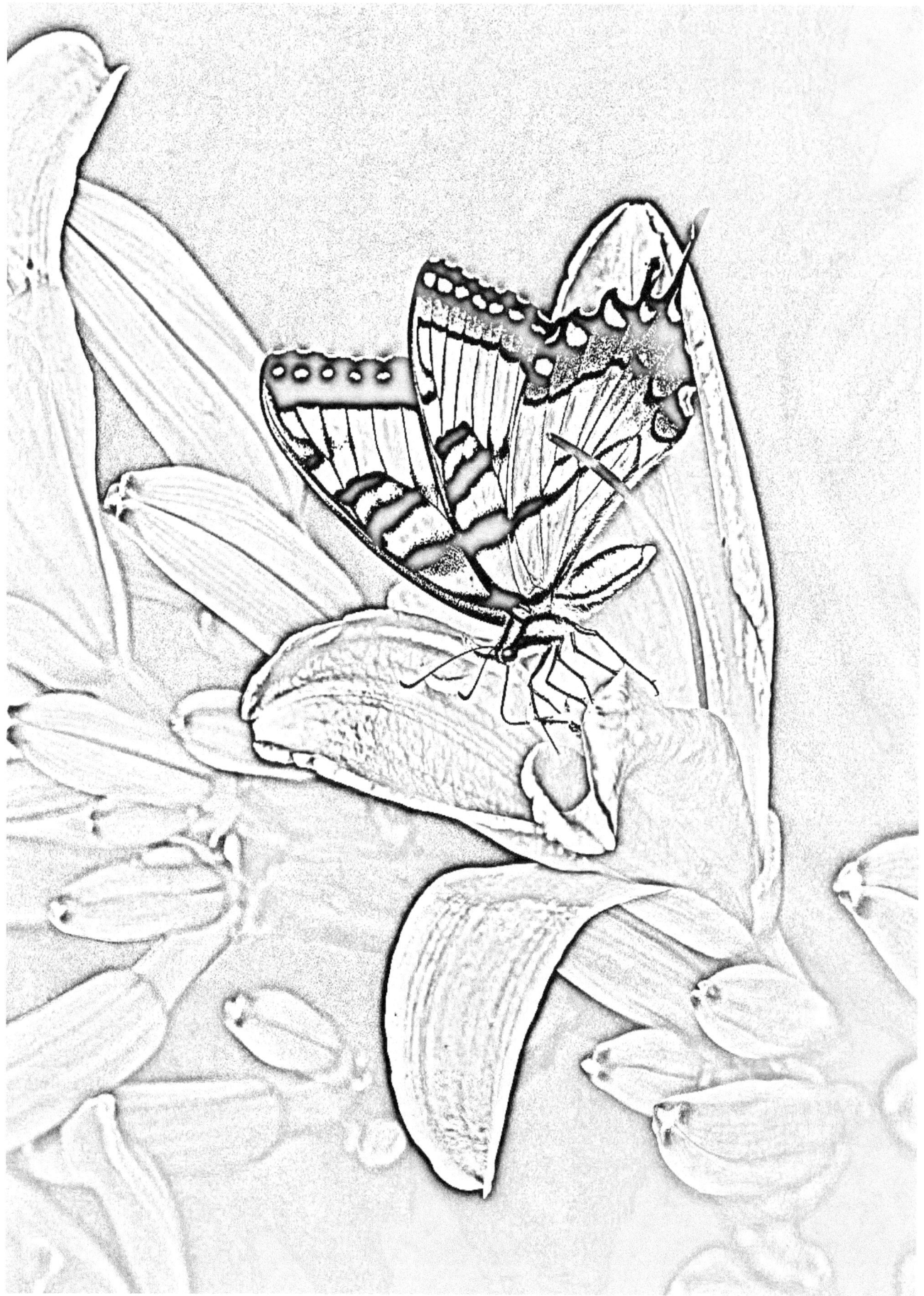

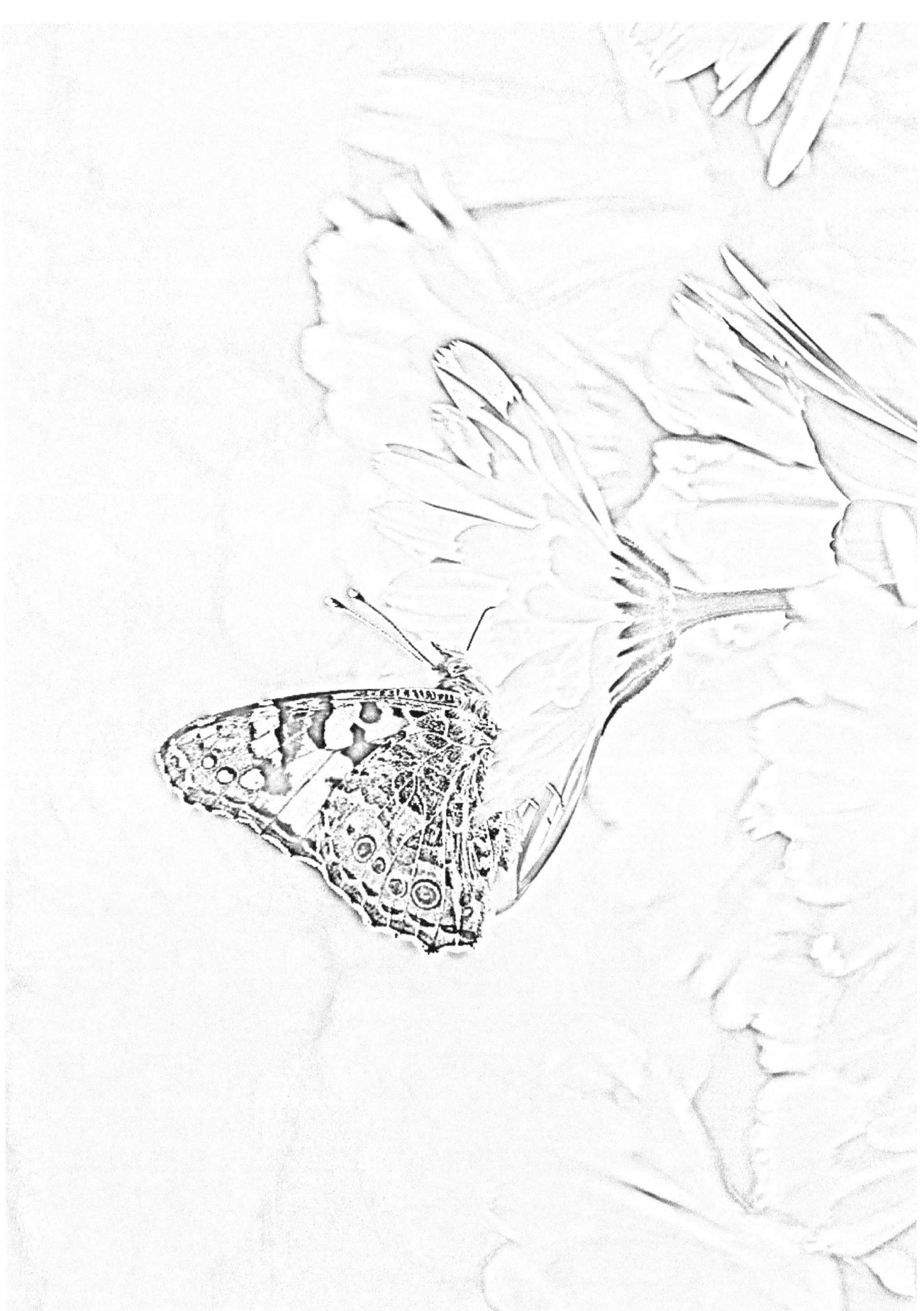

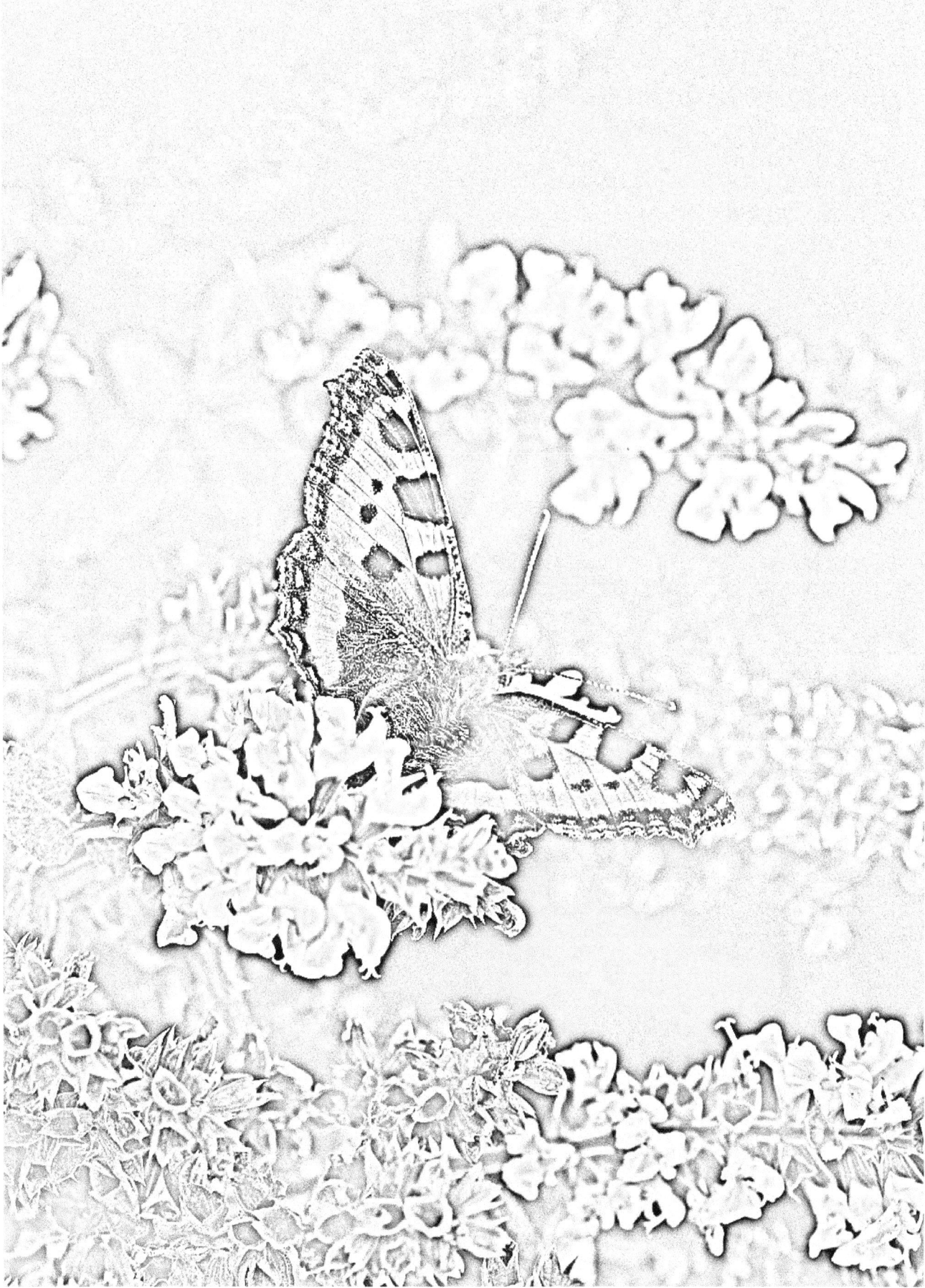

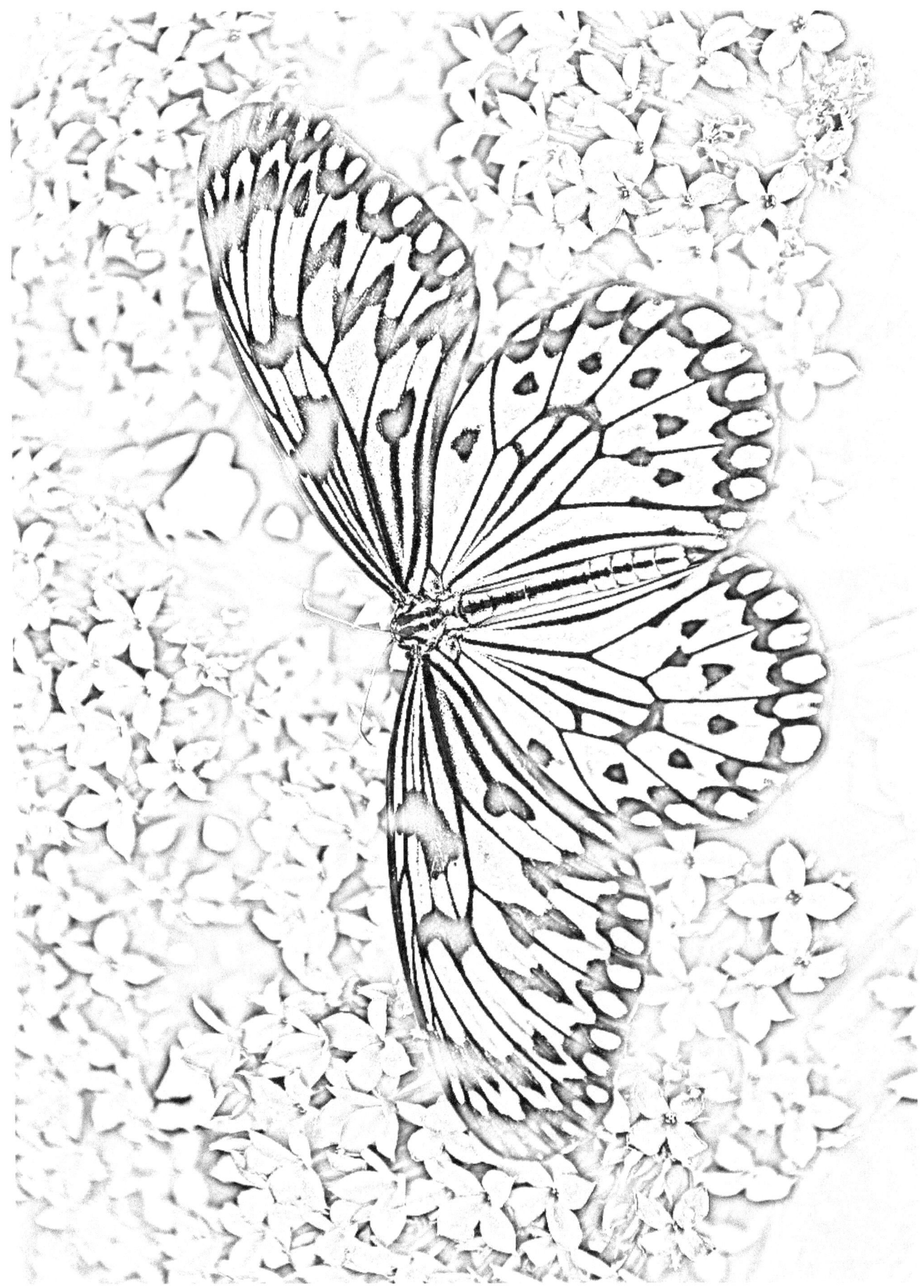

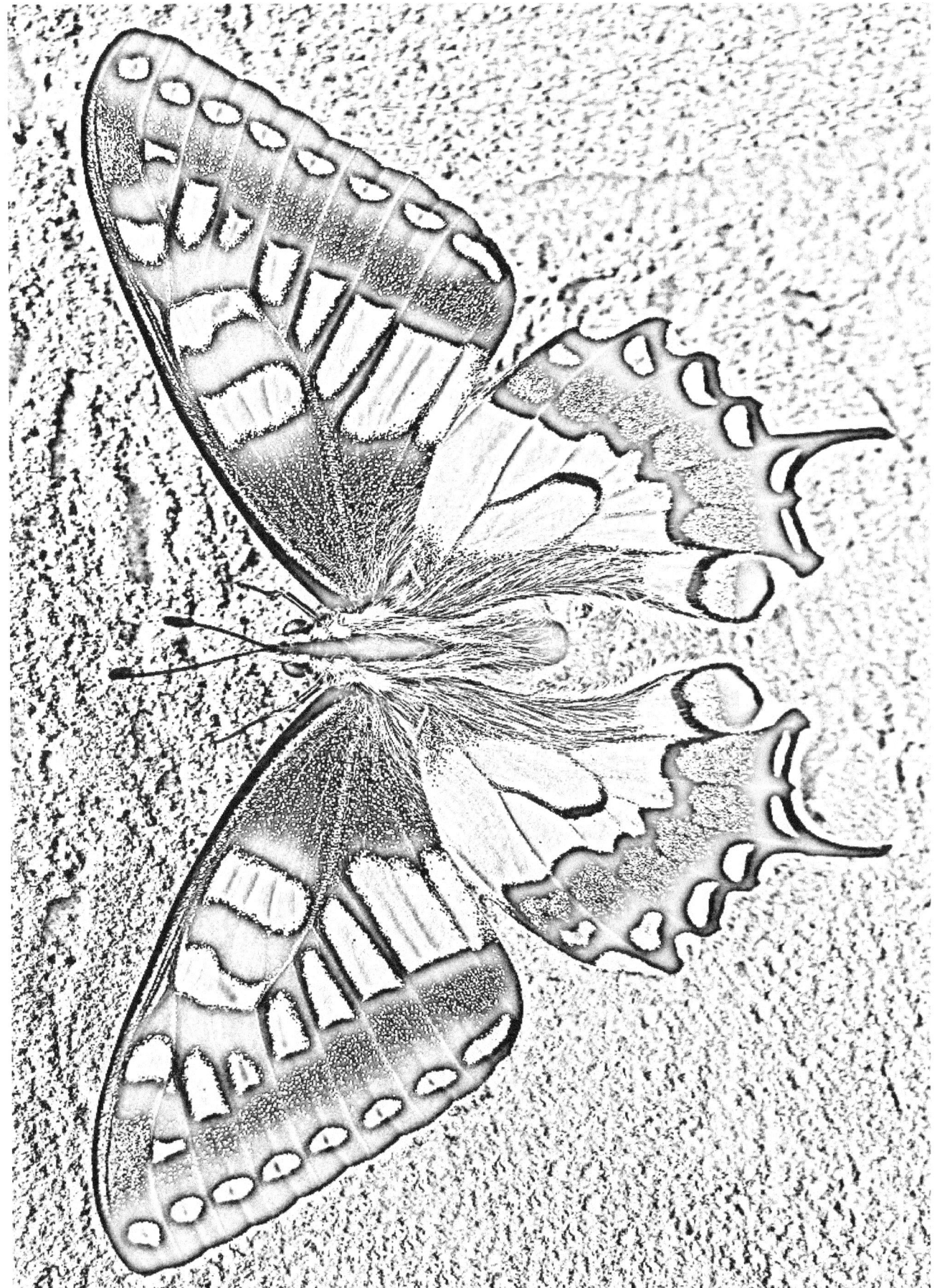

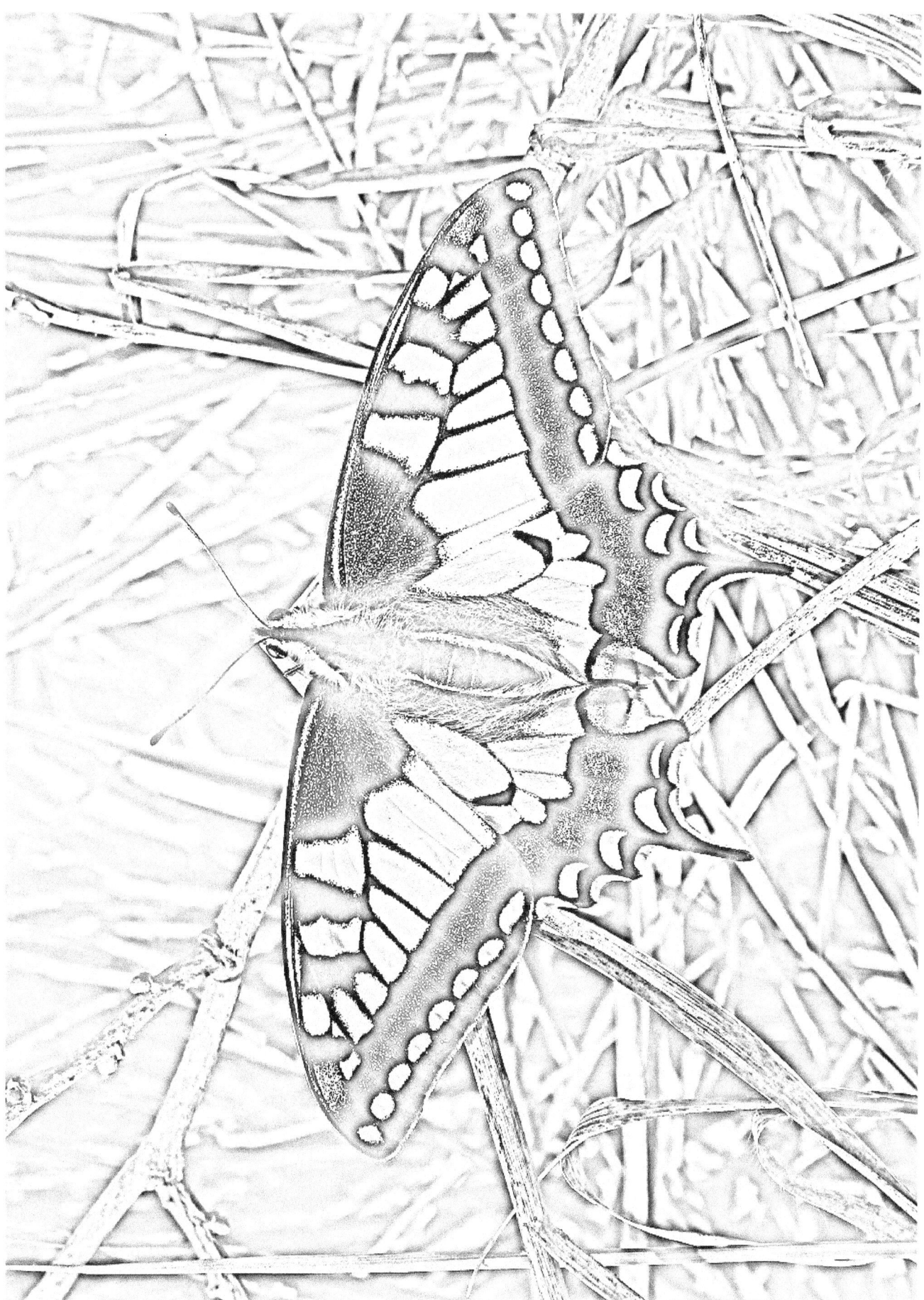

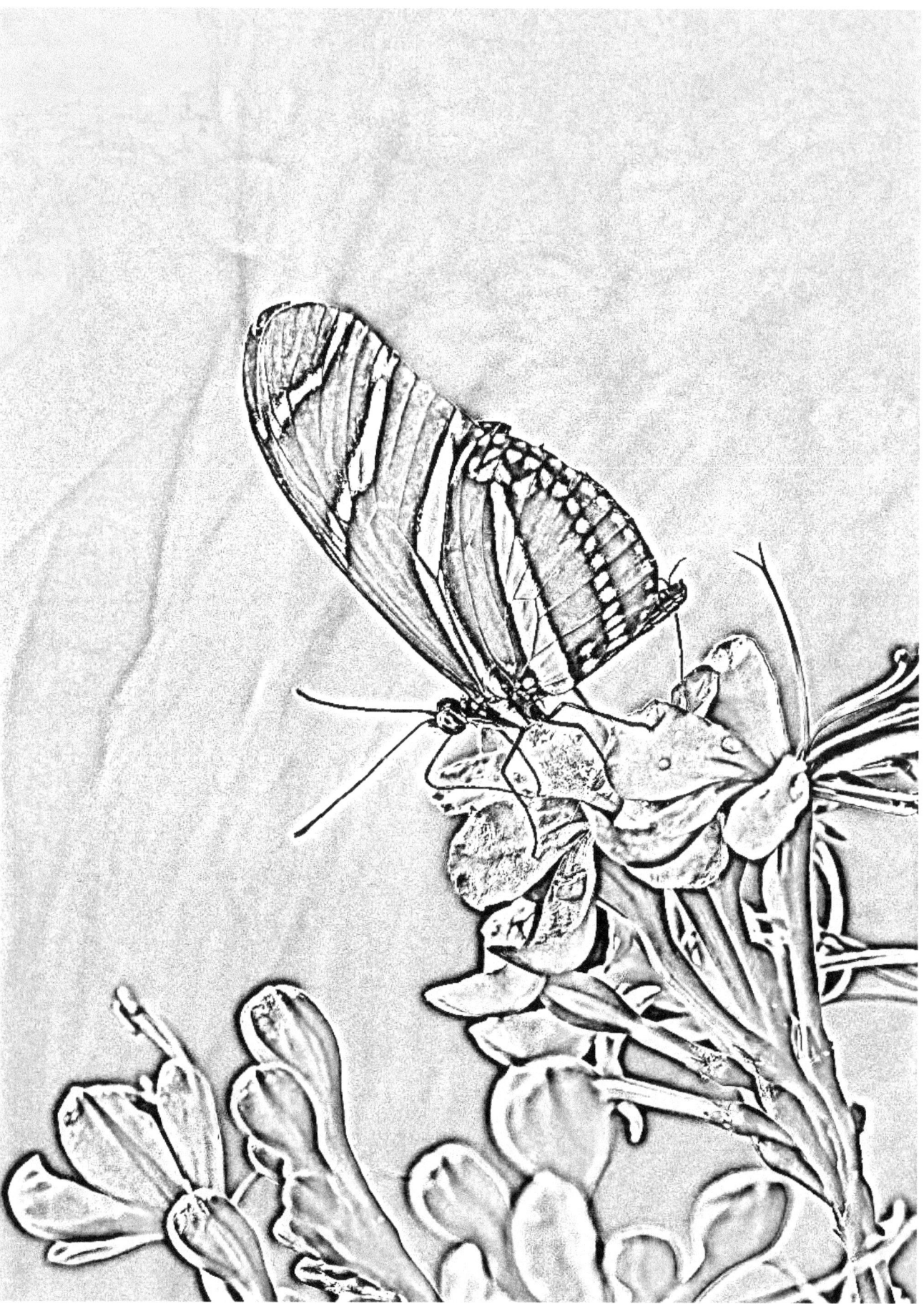

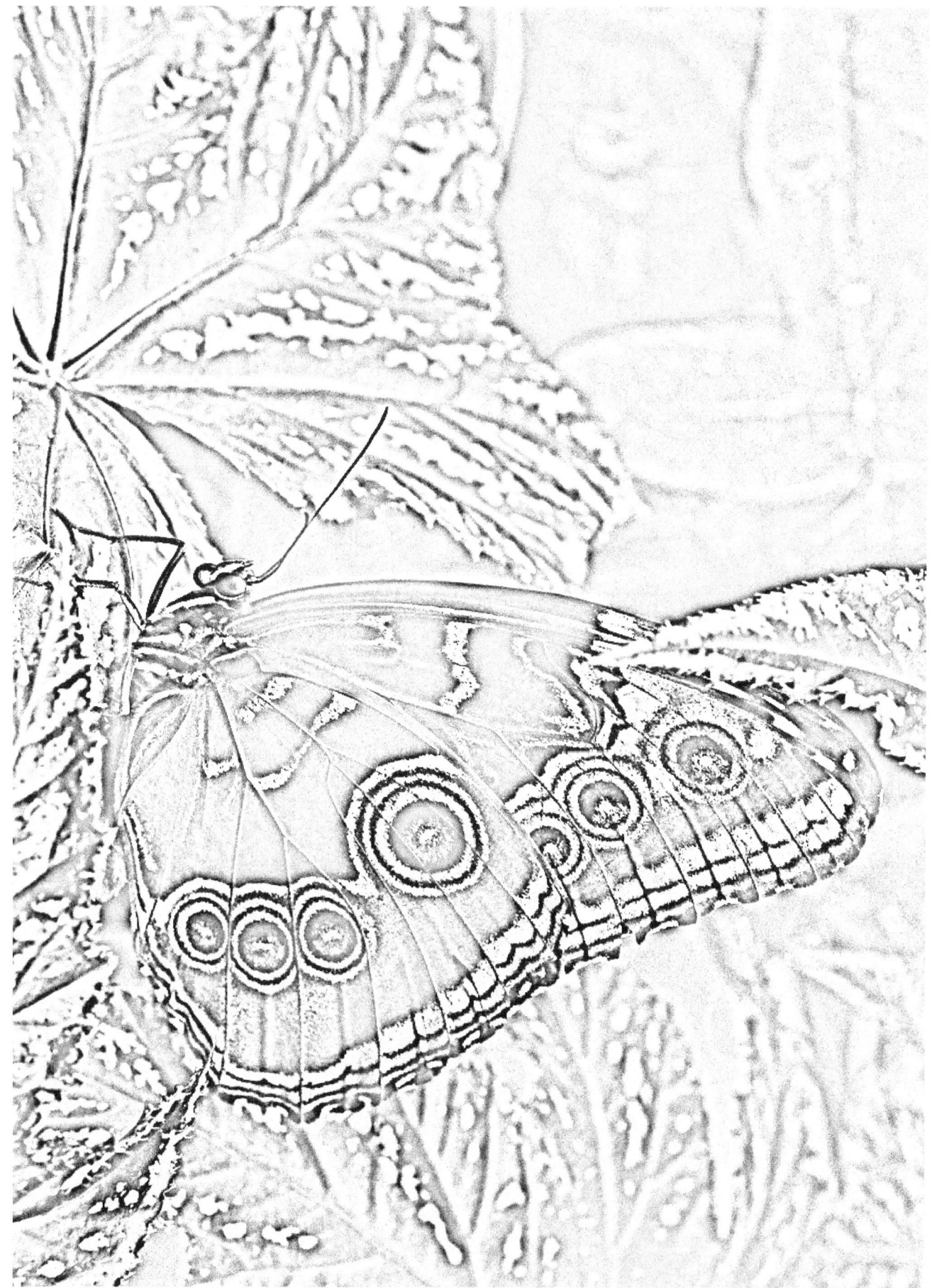

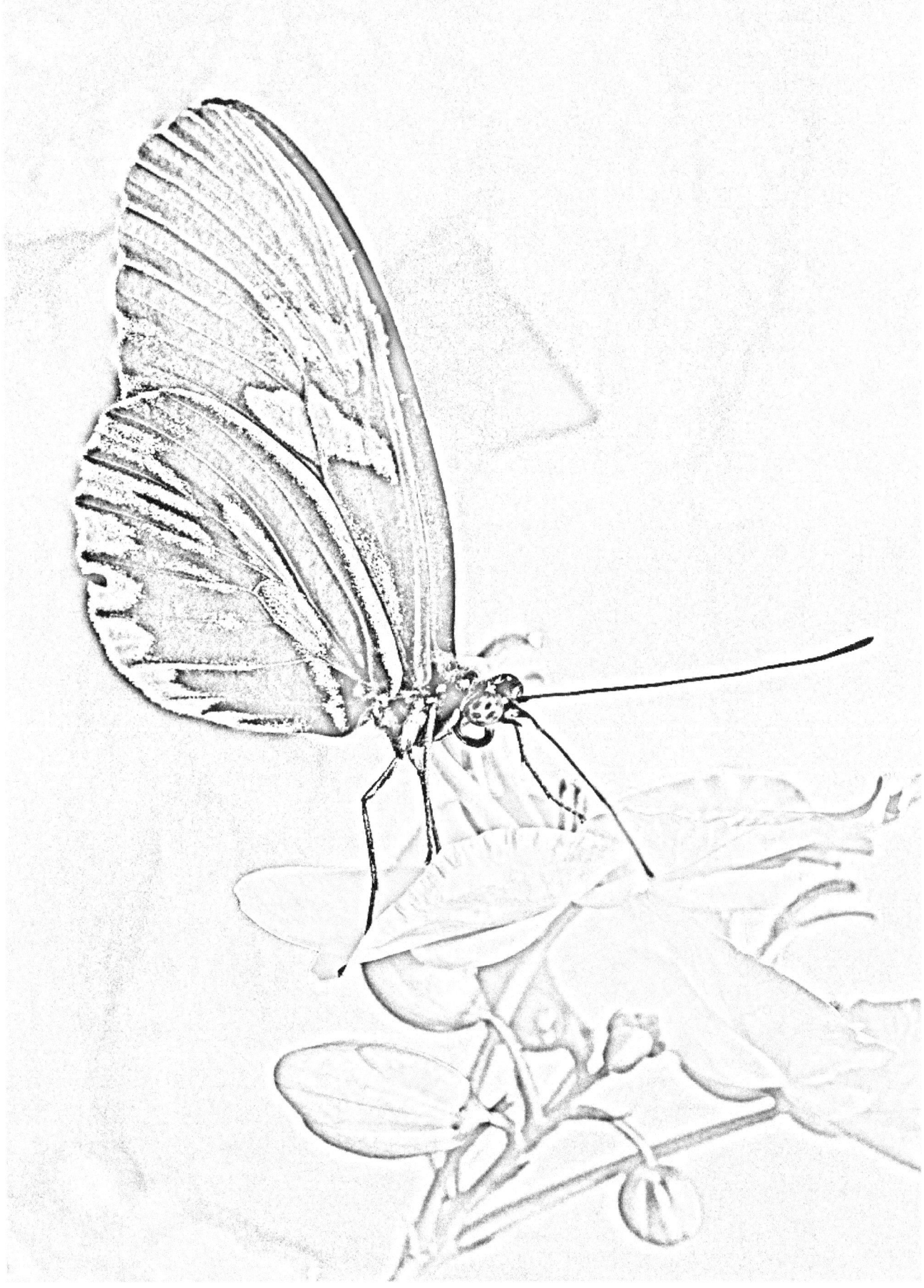

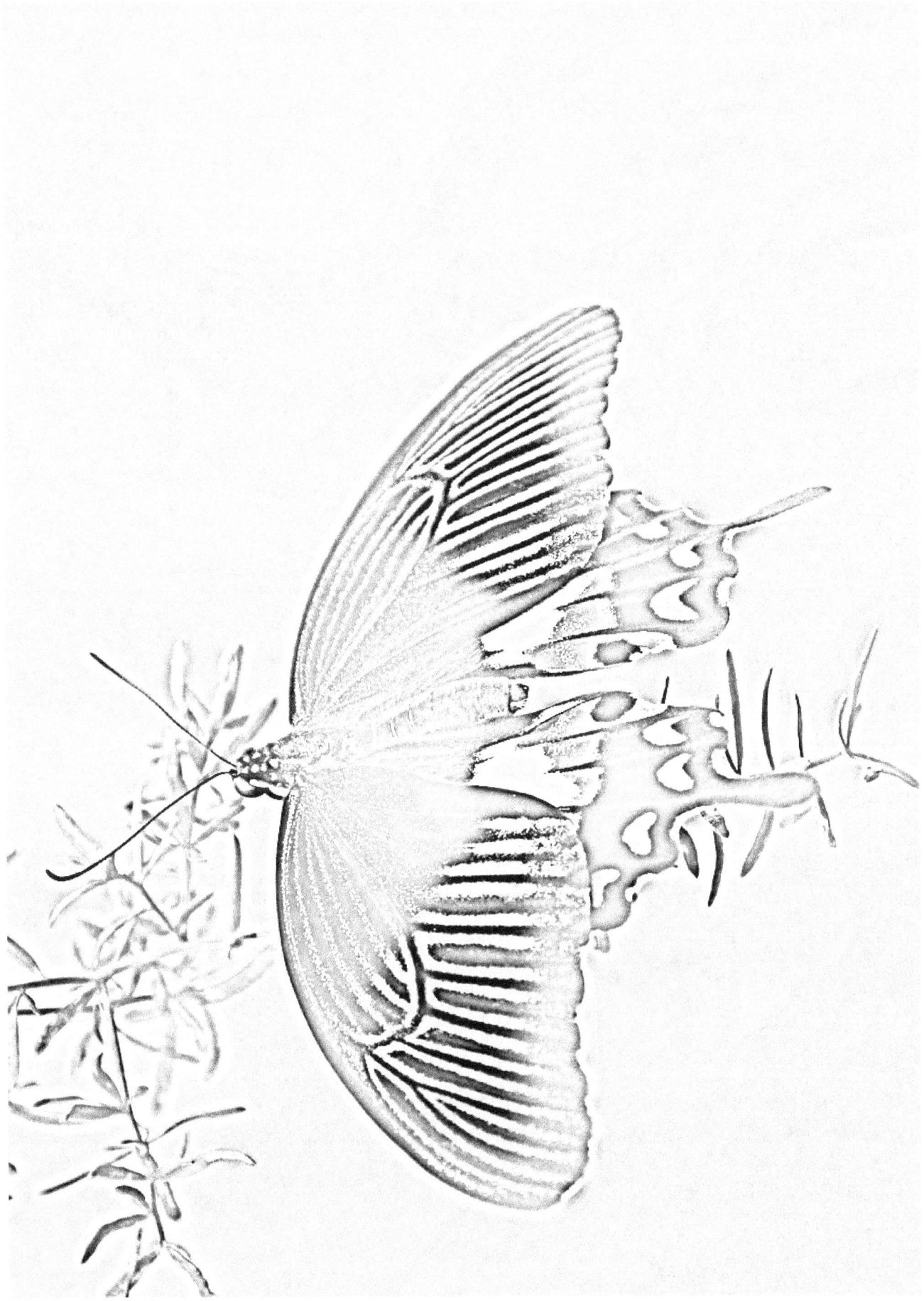

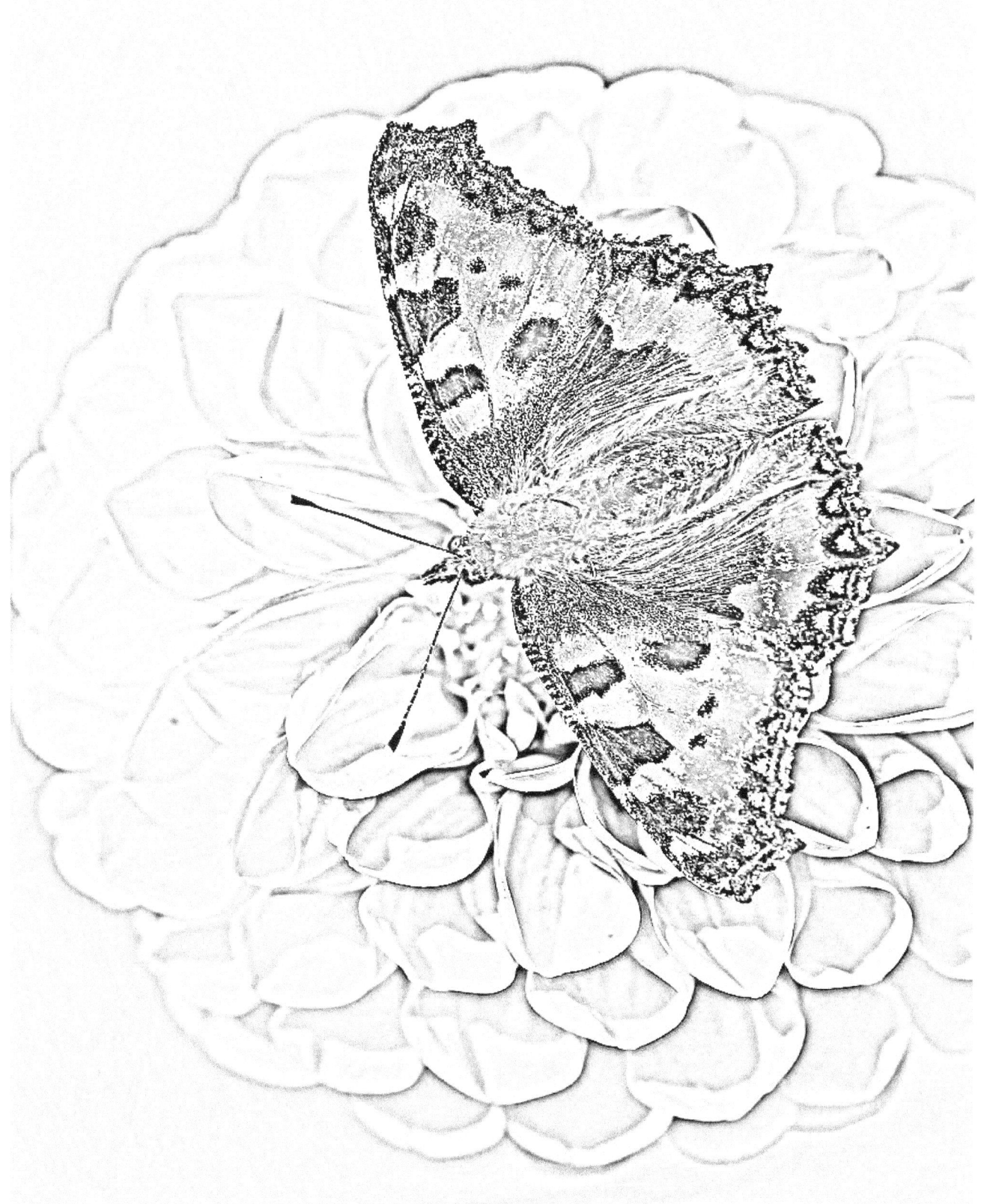

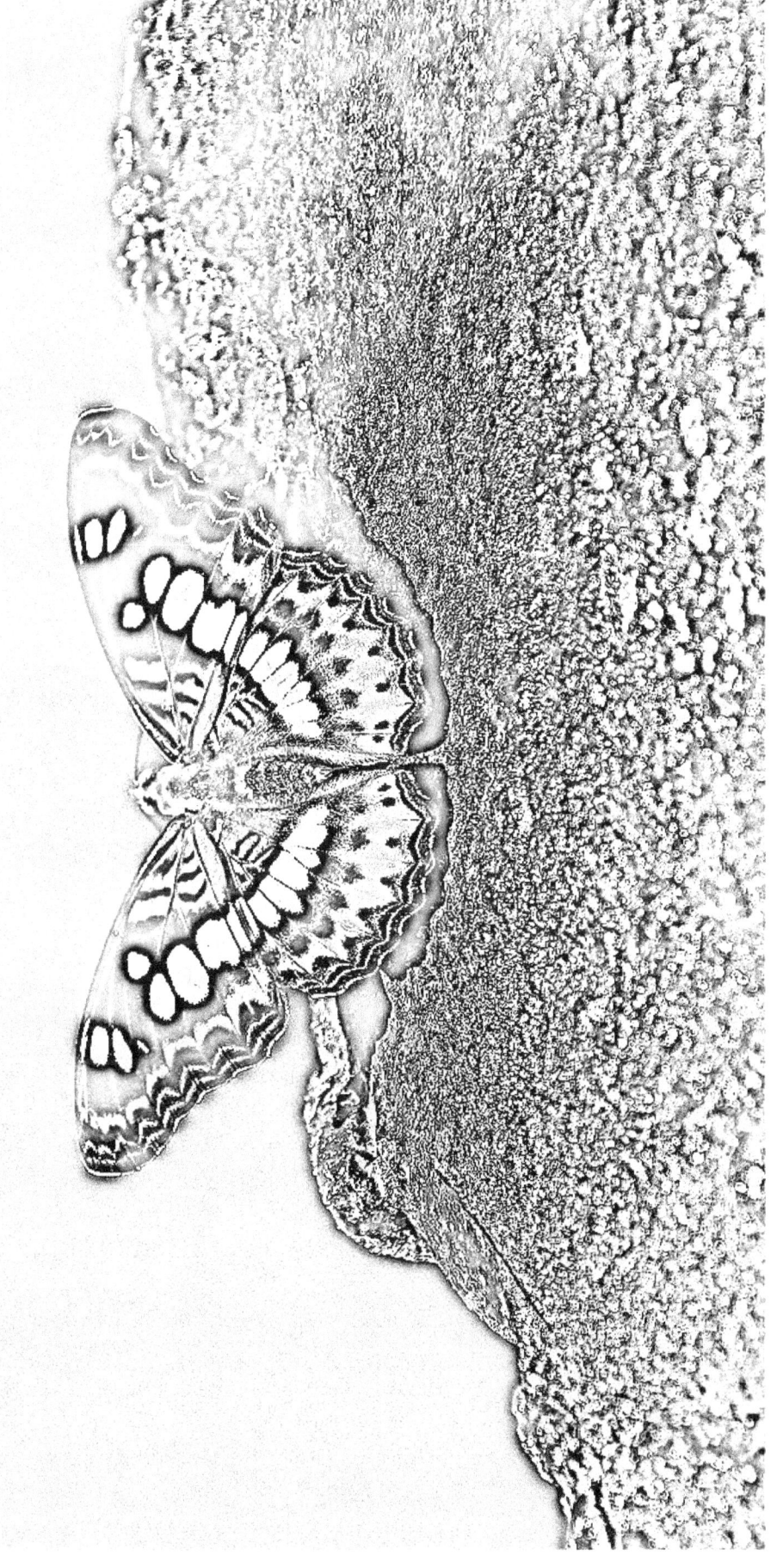

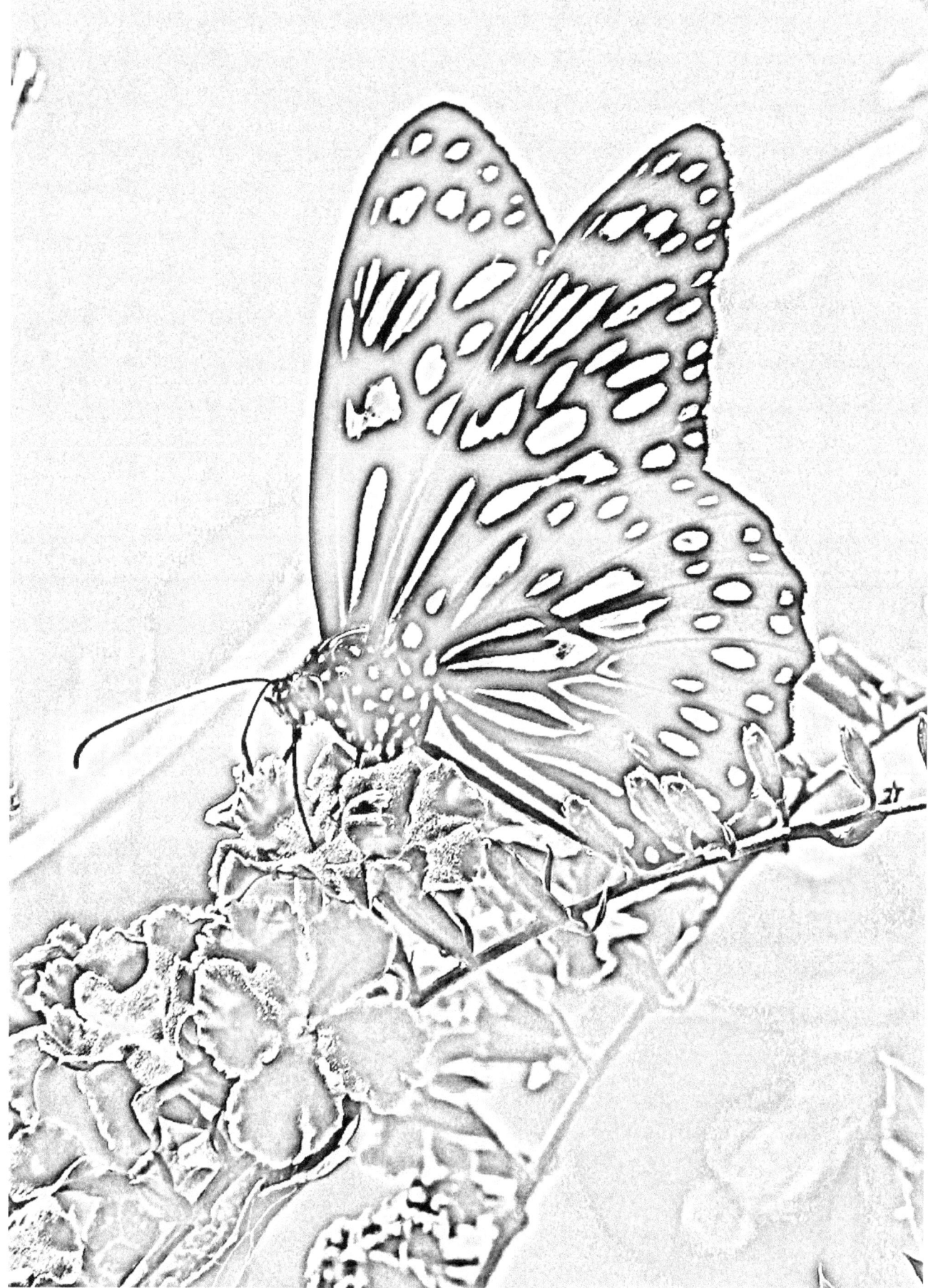

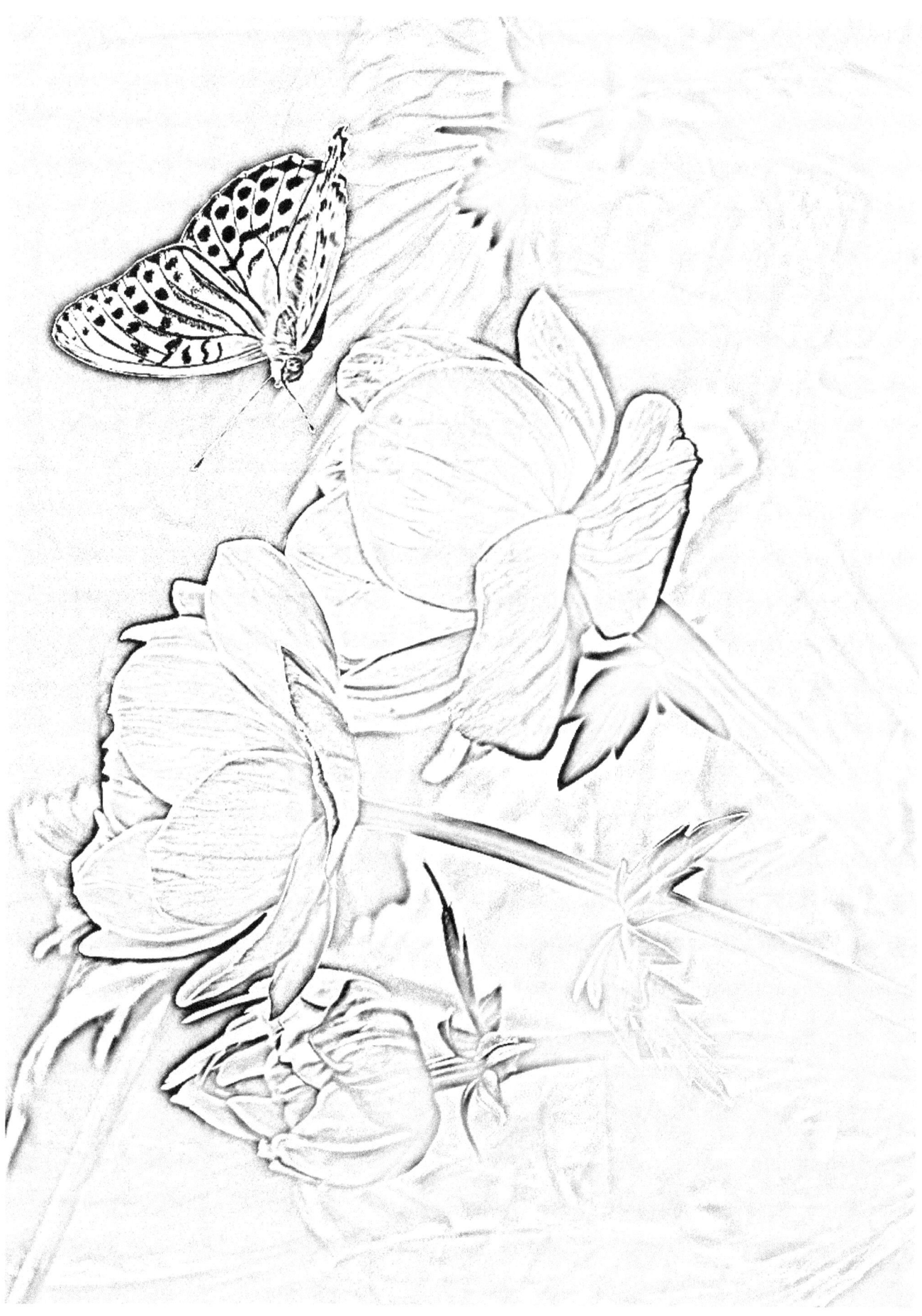

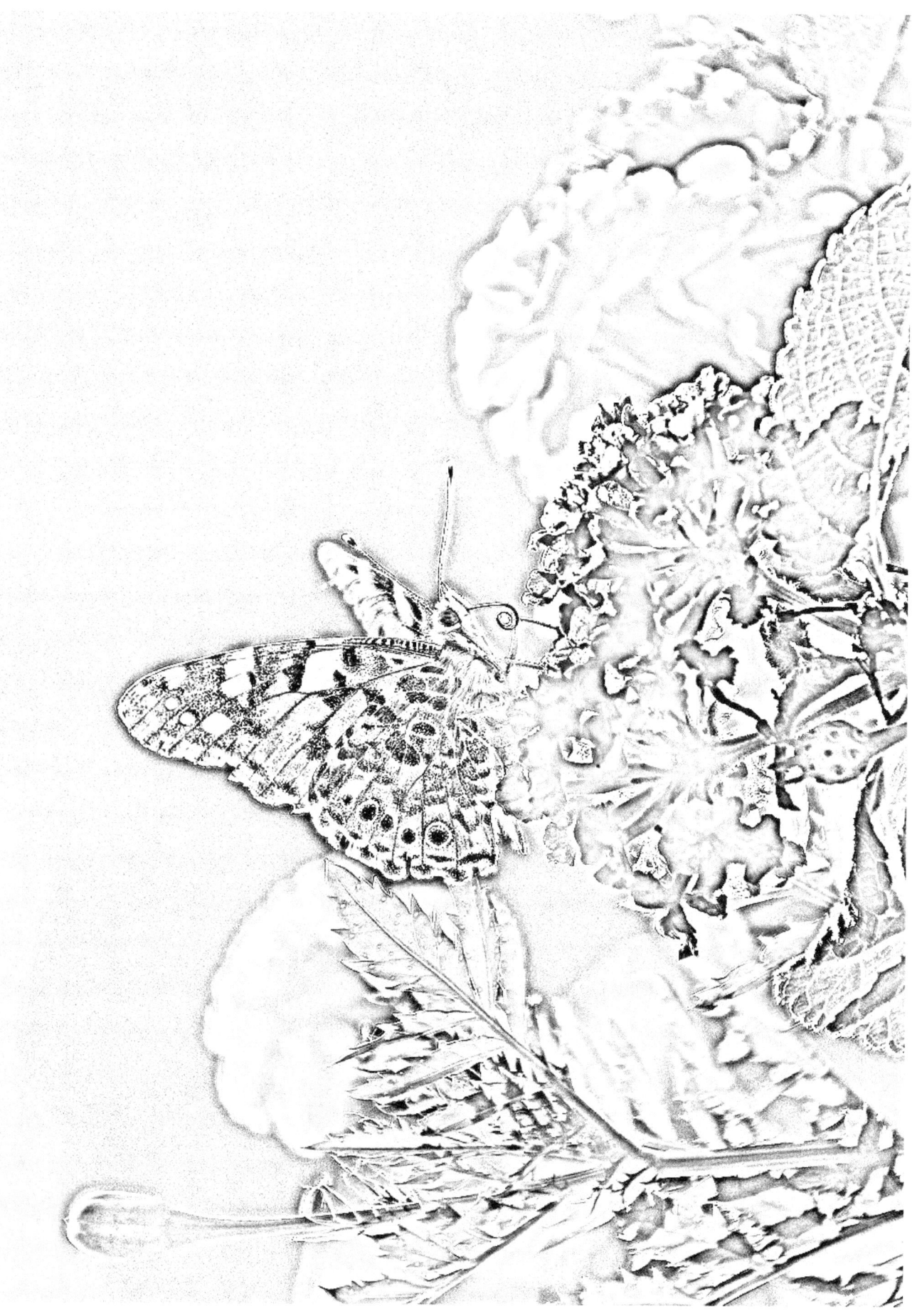

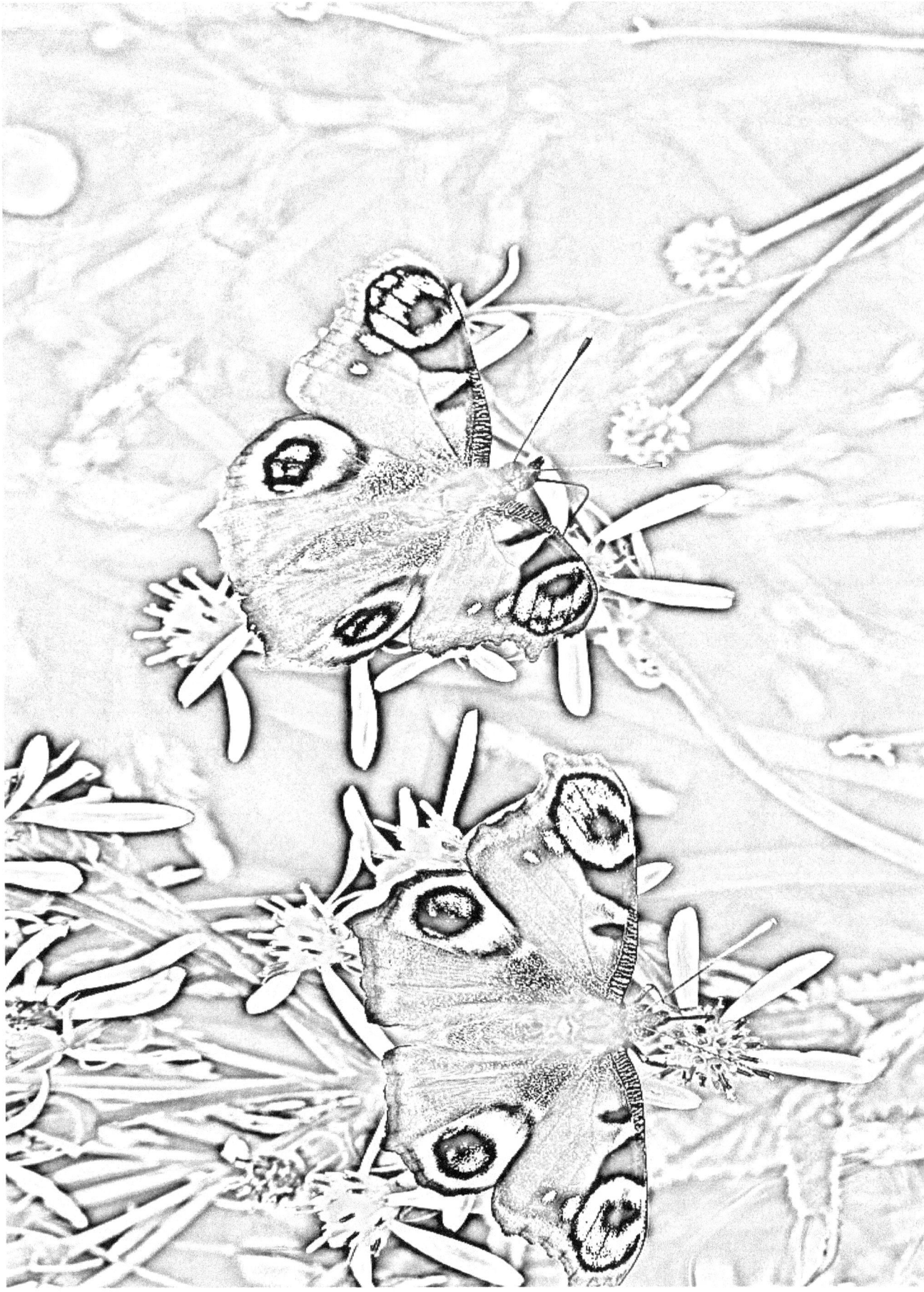

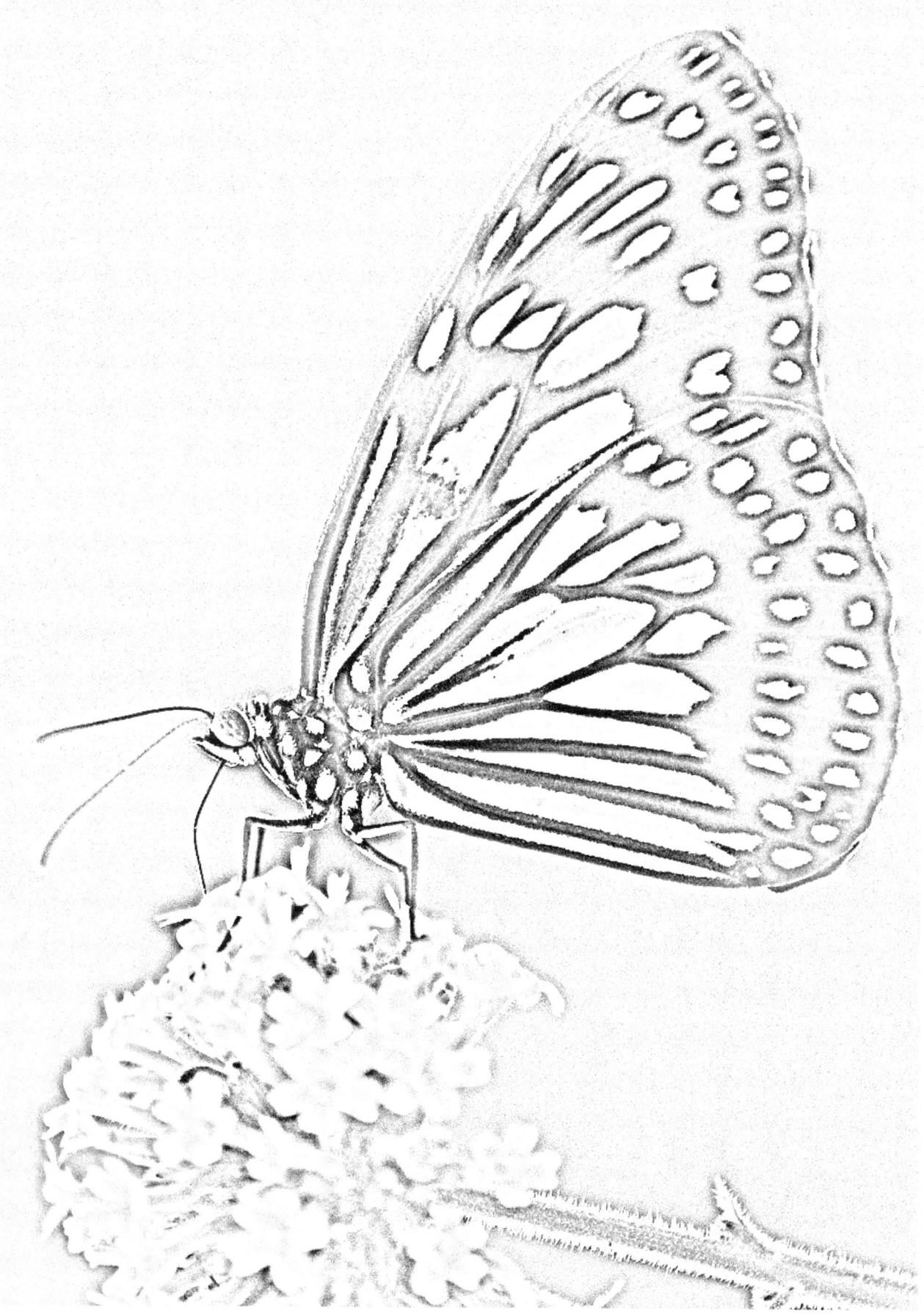

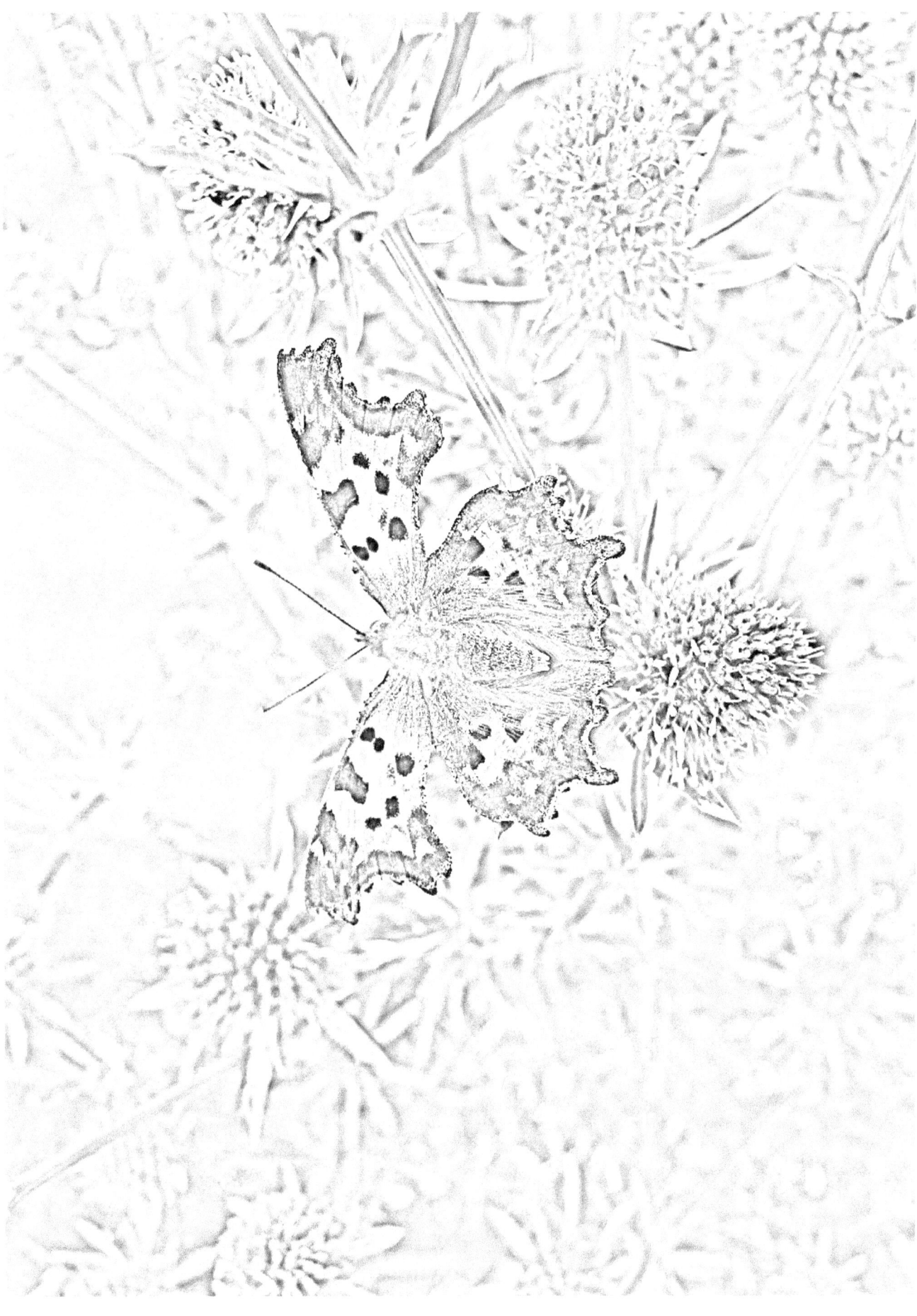

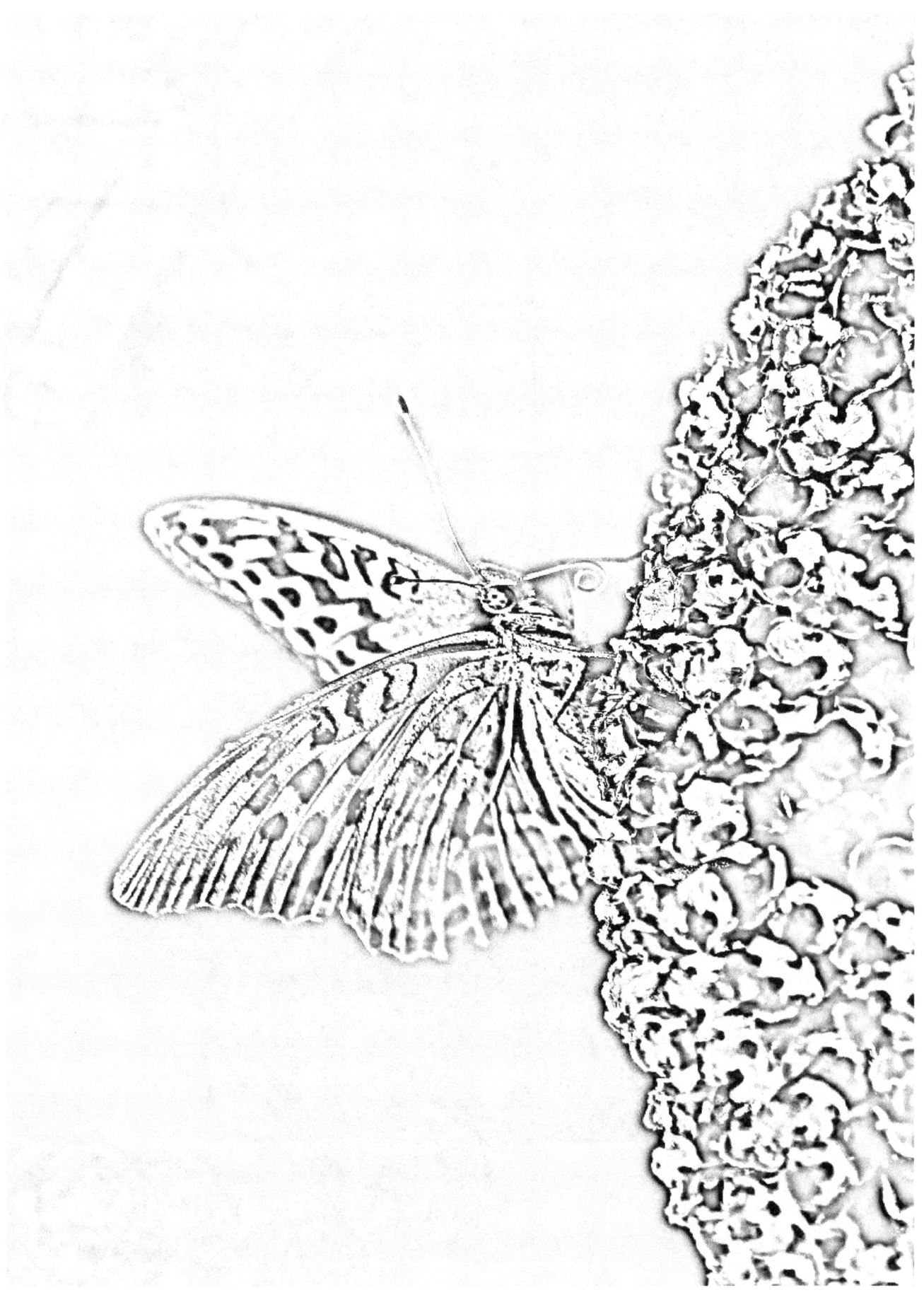

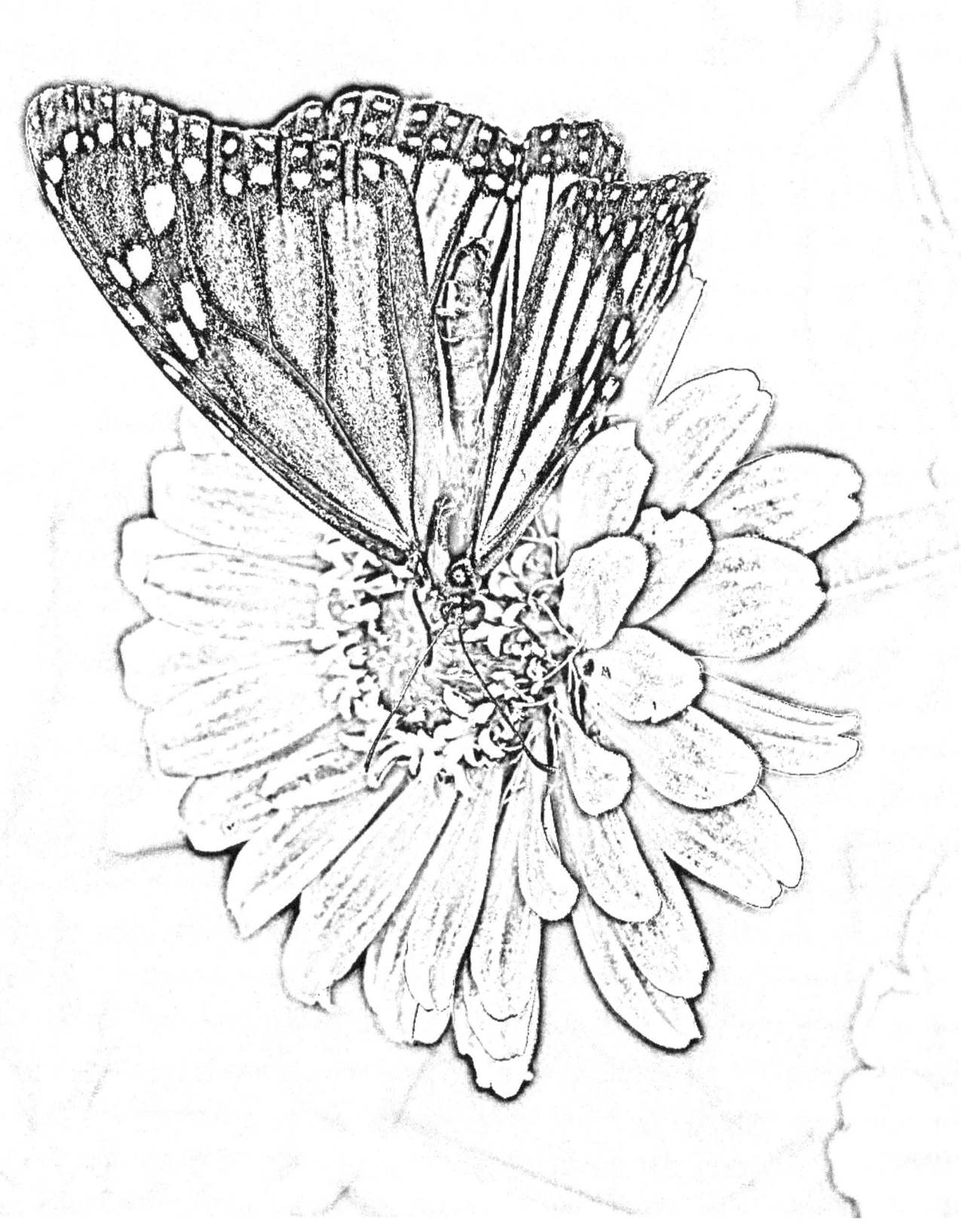

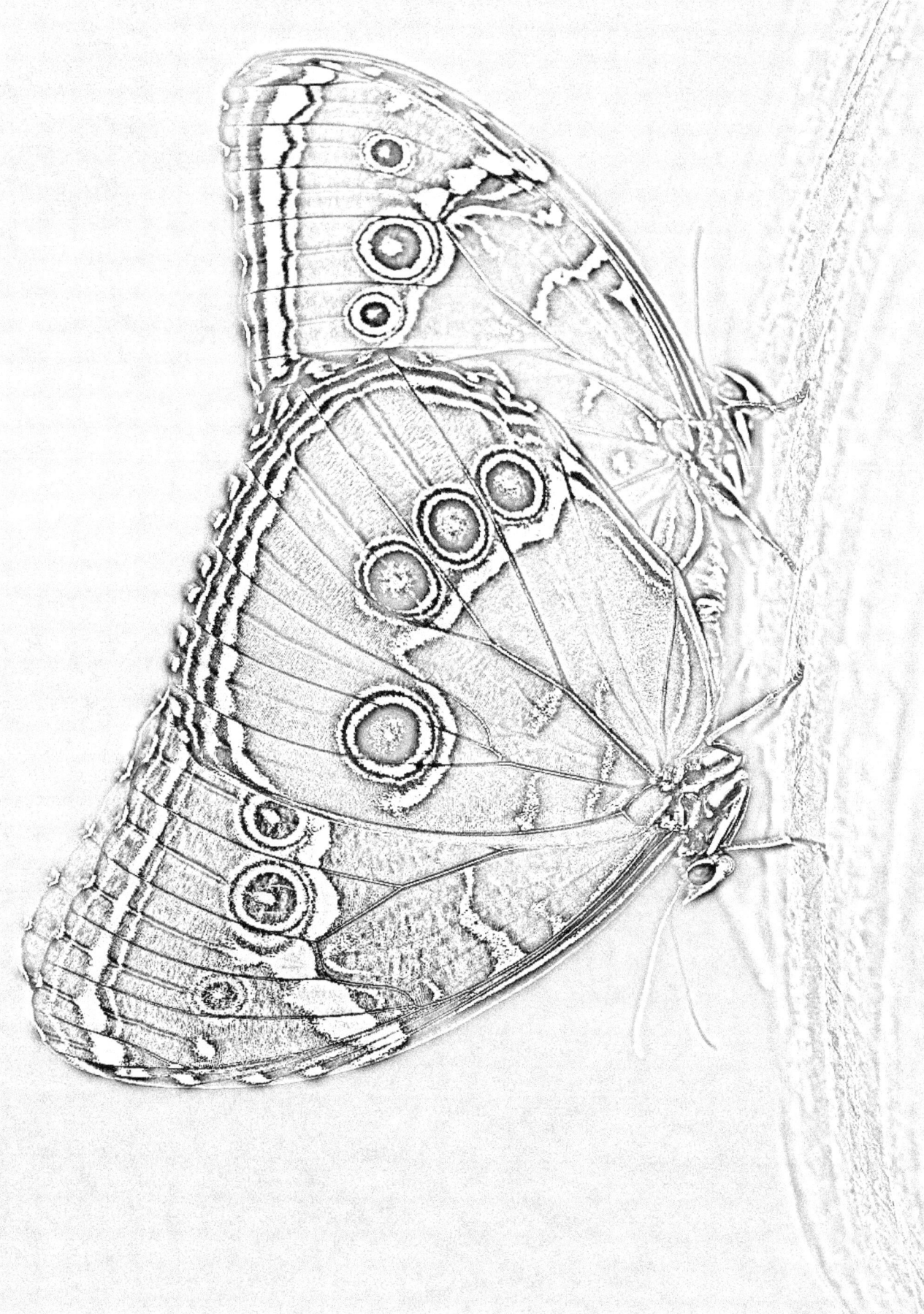

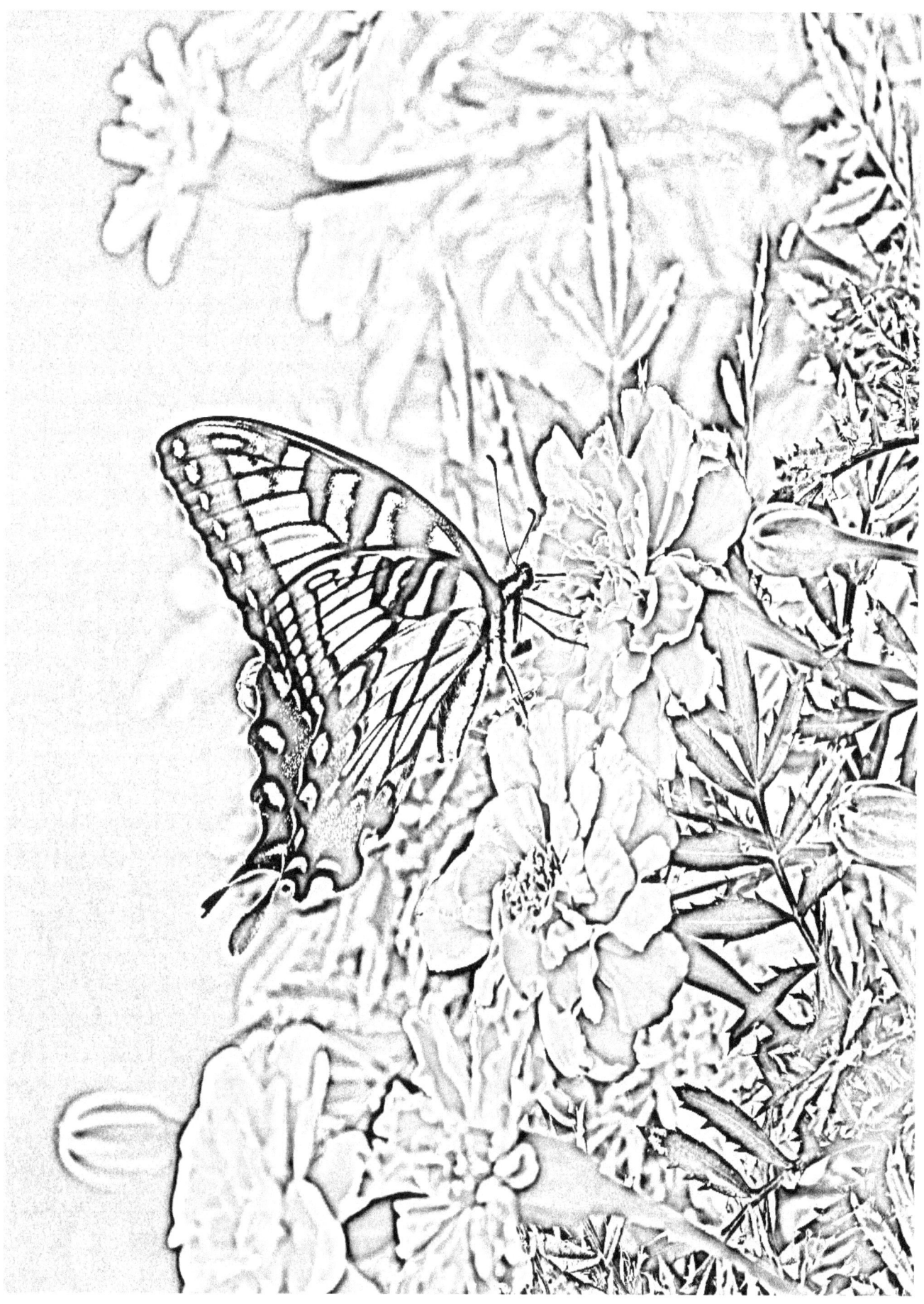

Thank You!

We hope you enjoyed our coloring book.

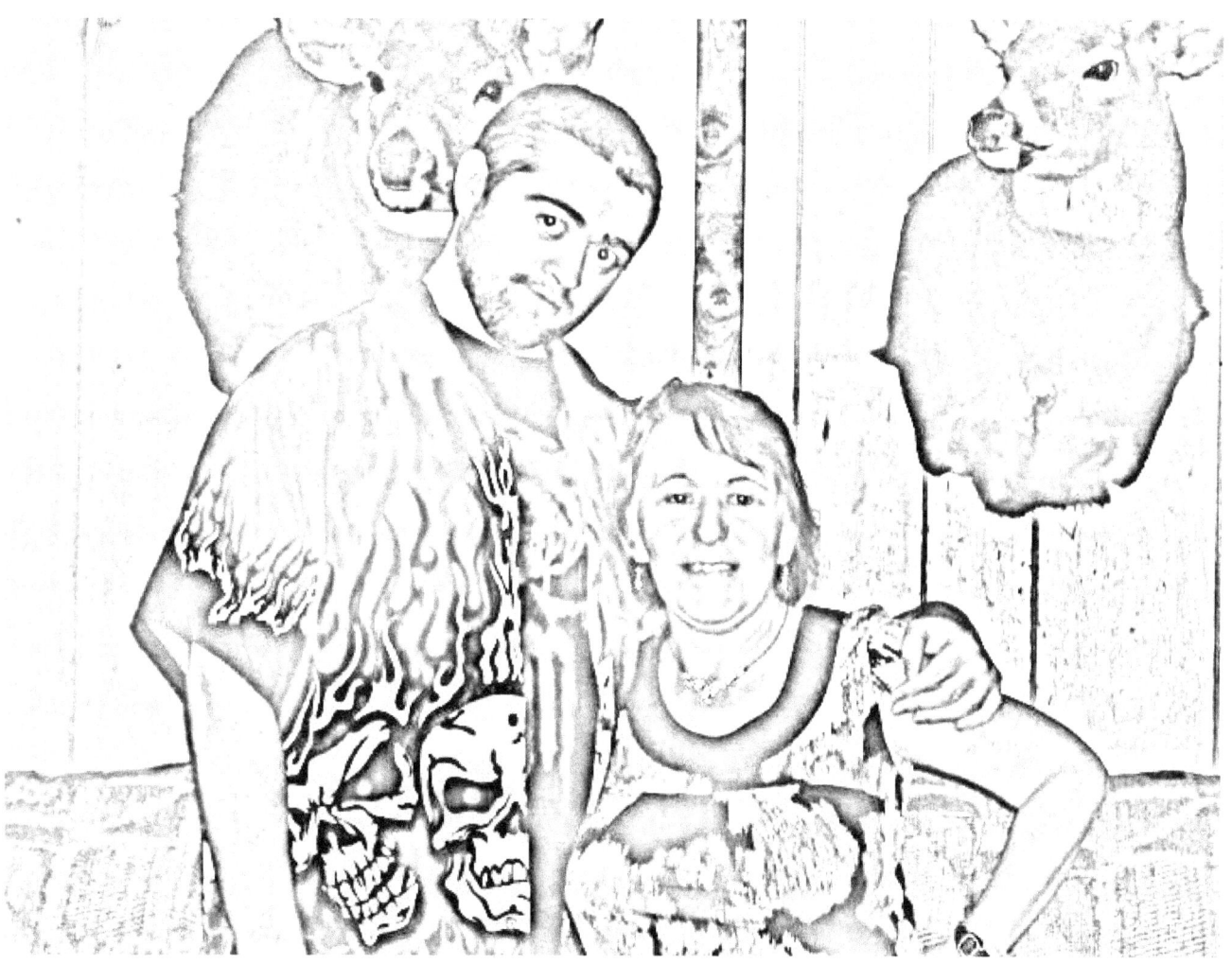

Watch for more color books from ARN Arts LLC.

Visit us at http://arnarts.wixsite.com/books

www.ingramcontent.com/pod-product-compliance
Lightning Source LLC
Chambersburg PA
CBHW081123180526
45170CB00008B/2984